Year Round Solar Greenhouse

Step-By-Step Guide to Design
And Build Your Own Passive
Solar Greenhouse in as Little as 30
Days Without Drowning in a Sea
of Technical Jargon

Small Footprint Press

various sources. Please consult a licensed professional before attempting any techniques outlined in this book.

By reading this document, the reader agrees that under no circumstances is the author responsible for any losses, direct or indirect, that are incurred as a result of the use of the information contained within this document, including, but not limited to, errors, omissions, or inaccuracies.

Table of Contents

Introduction

"The glorious lamp of heaven, the sun."

–by Robert Herrick

The world is just not what it used to be. Everyone knows this. Taking a look outside or a walk on the beach reflects the vast differences between today and ten years ago. Even going to a mall and checking out the food on the shelf will tell you a lot. Life has become so modernized, wiping out the existence of self-sustaining farms or gardens in exchange for massive, industrialized, and processed foods. Anyone who has grown their produce can show you the radical difference between plants grown by the earth and sun, untouched by chemicals in comparison to those in the shops—significantly smaller, tasteless, and pumped with substances whose damage is unknown.

You may have been inspired to take on gardening. You may have the desire to build your greenhouse to transform back into an individual who is self-sufficient, going against society's food standards in exchange for quality, fresh produce. You may also have a love for plants and a green thumb, enjoying the tranquility and joy that comes with gardening. It is certainly a rewarding experience, and now the future is truly at your fingertips. Greenhouse gardening is surely on another level than what is normally done, and its popularity is growing at a rapid rate.

Knowing where to start and what you need is tricky. You have probably heard of passive solar greenhouses and even considered trying it yourself, but without proper and updated guidance or care, there is a certain fear of failure. There are a lot of reasons for starting a greenhouse. Perhaps you want to be ensured that your plants will grow as well as have everything operating as smoothly as possible. You may have a tight budget and space. You may also want to build a greenhouse due to your harsh climate that does not allow the growth of plants in your normal hostile environment, where it rains too much or is far too cold. Wintertime might just be the bane of your existence, as it wipes out most of your plants in the frost and snow. You also want to be completely sure that your project will not fail.

This book acts as a constructive, helpful guide for anyone who wants to build a solar greenhouse in thirty days, going in-depth on how to build it as well as tips and tools for the building process. It is a helping hand and simplifies complicated instructions to make your DIY journey more straightforward and more enjoyable. It will tackle all issues you may encounter, such as budget constraints, climate concerns, choosing a type of greenhouse, ventilation, and more. It may sound like a lot, but the reward will be worth it. Not only will a solar greenhouse turn an environmentally hostile space into a plant-friendly haven, but it also will have a practical build to combat the different seasons that come across your path.

Small Footprint Press was born out of frustration with the current state of the planet. Our mission is to help you sustainably survive and thrive while ensuring together that the world is a better place for future generations to come. Living more sustainably is a win for both humans and the environment, allowing the world to prosper alongside humanity. If more people went green, the world would be a happier, healthier, and more sustainable place, where one can see blue skies, clear waters, and a blooming ecosystem. A passive solar greenhouse combats the over industrialized and commercialized food system, where people are completely reliant on mass productions. However, with mass production comes mass waste. A greenhouse's very intention is to eliminate waste and recycle as much as possible.

The idea and inspiration to build a solar greenhouse brings you one step closer to creating a better world. It may seem insignificant to the actions of a single person. Yet, that is all it takes to instigate another's actions and ultimately building up a community of like-minded people. After all, you will be eating healthier foods and exposing yourself to higher levels of oxygen produced by your greenhouse in the long run.

Chapter 1:
What Is a Passive Solar Greenhouse?

Aesthetic Greenhouse

You may have a general idea of a solar greenhouse. The terms solar and greenhouse form an explanation in and of itself. Yet when going in detail, it can be pretty confusing or unclear. So, what exactly does it mean to have a passive solar greenhouse?

A passive solar greenhouse relies on two main factors: solar radiation and ideal growing conditions. Solar radiation is necessary for plants to create photosynthesis as well as survive. Plants need good conditions, such as constant temperature and humidity, to grow. An average greenhouse does manage to keep the conditions relatively the same, but, come winter, fuel is usually needed to keep up the sustenance. Energy is not only costly but also a high pollutant factor. Therefore, the average greenhouse might keep the pests away but is also bound to the seasons.

When a greenhouse is solar, the entire structure will heat up through the use of sunlight. It means that adding fuel is duly unnecessary. The passive solar greenhouse soaks in the sunlight during the winter season. Then, it will create proper heating and solar radiation for plants to thrive in the winter as they did in the summer.

Active Solar Greenhouse vs. Passive Solar Greenhouse

There are various types of greenhouses, but since we explicitly focus on passive solar greenhouses, it would be wise to know the difference between passive and active solar greenhouses. They are both solar, which means they derive and take energy from the sun. However, they also serve more designated purposes. Being solar-driven means that they can harness the power and store it for the colder nights and seasons.

These solar greenhouses can be classified into two different categories. One is known to be active, while the other is passive.

An active solar greenhouse tends to use extra energy. This means it moves the energy from a storage area to some other regions of an operational solar greenhouse.

However, a passive solar greenhouse tends to focus more on storing in preparation for the weather that tends to stay colder for longer. This is specifically ideal for people who want a cost-effective method to grow crops all year long.

Principles of Operation

There are some general principles on which a greenhouse operates. It first of all relies on the storage of solar energy that was accumulated through the day. The second step is where the greenhouse releases the energy gradually during the evening and winter.

A maximum amount of solar radiation (heat) is collected throughout the day and stored. Then, the heat is released into the interior. The loss of heat is reduced due to the insulation built inside the greenhouse. However, one also builds in ventilation to prevent overheating occurring. Therefore, it compensates for both extremes of heat and cold. However, it is a delicate balance, and this is where the science and tricky part comes in. Working out the balance is ultimately the key to creating a flourishing greenhouse, one whose temperature's swings at a reasonable rate to create a peaceful and amicable environment for plants to simply thrive. There are several steps a person can indeed take to achieve this.

Advantages of Passive Solar Greenhouses

To be motivated for a project such as this, it is best to understand what it brings to the table. A passive solar greenhouse is different from an average greenhouse for several reasons, bringing multiple benefits for you to enjoy.

- First, a passive solar greenhouse does absorb and release the necessary amount of solar radiation for the photosynthesis process that needs to occur for plants. The plants need a good amount of sunlight to survive properly.

- A significant reduction in heat loss considering a greenhouse has thick, triple-layered walls built-in from north, west, and east sides. This helps to keep the plants nice and cozy during the winter.

- There is constant sustenance of the climatic conditions in the house. It means a person is capable of growing vegetables all year round regardless of the weather. This factor saves a lot of time and reduces the need to always visit the grocery store for certain vegetables when it is out of season. For people who love gardening, this is ideal, considering they do not have to wait to plant their seeds nor struggle to grow what they want to.

- It is also an income possibility, especially if you are in a rural population selling your fresh produce. You may be surprised how many people would instead opt for homegrown produce rather than those sold in the local store, as they are fresher, healthier, and certainly not pumped with excessive chemicals.

- The design and build of a passive solar greenhouse are practical, built alongside the east-west axis (later explained in the book), which allows the greenhouse to soak in the sun for the most prolonged period.

- Any needs for specific vegetables that are not ordinarily sustainable or capable of being grown can be fulfilled in a passive solar greenhouse. For example, if you would like to produce foods that cannot even typically be grown in your country, it is quite possible to do so in a greenhouse.

- The materials necessary to create a passive solar greenhouse are, on average, locally available. Considering it is made out of straw, wood, and stone. The only abnormality would be the transparent glass or cover sheet, which happens to cover the south side of the wall. These are called glazings and are an essential aspect of your greenhouse.

- The greenhouse doesn't need special licensed people to build it. If you know enough about construction or want to hire a local builder, you are more than welcome. The only people you may need to call in are licensed plumbers or electricians only if absolutely need be.

- The original investment costs can be recovered after three years if the production is managed professionally and the product is sold. Otherwise, you can consider the money you are saving from not going grocery shopping as a return of investment.

- The costs are relatively modest. It all depends on what and how you install it. You can undoubtedly opt for cheap options to even recycling items that you already have.

- The heat source relies entirely on the sun and material to heat the water and hold material such as concrete. The energy source is altogether economical as well as accessible. You will be cutting a lot of costs of fuel and electricity from simply building a solar greenhouse. However, if your climate is known to be abnormally frigid with little sun exposure, you may have to compensate a little for that. So this benefit does depend entirely on where you stay.

Four Main Elements of a Passive Solar Greenhouse

To understand the basics of a passive solar greenhouse, you need to know the four main elements of the greenhouse. They are the foundational building blocks and the keys to success. Therefore, when planning to build your greenhouse, these are by far the elements you need to consider first and plan in detail before moving to actual construction.

Orientation

The first element is orientation. This is the greenhouse position to reach maximum exposure to the sun for the most extended period possible. The design starts with choosing the proper orientation of your greenhouse. If you are in the Northern Hemisphere, it means you need to maximize the exposure of your greenhouse on the southern side. Whereas if you are in the southern hemisphere, you need to maximize the exposure on the northern side of the house.

If you are in the northern hemisphere, then the north side of your greenhouse will collect the minimum amount of light. That is why some rooms in a house are colder than others. Therefore it is best to focus on insulating that side as best as you can in order to reduce the amount of heat loss that may occur. This might seem like common knowledge when building your greenhouses, yet there are still some questions and confusion that could arise when you are busily orientating your greenhouse.

The best location for your greenhouse is where there is full access to light, but it does need shade as well. Shading is not so important in the summer, where the trees can protect the greenhouse from the sun's harsh heat, but those same trees may block vital rays in the winter. This does mean it is better to build your greenhouse close to deciduous trees. Trees that lose their leaves in the winter, reducing the amount of shading, but helping it out in the summer when the leaves do grow back. While trees are useful for shading, you do not need to build next to trees, as you can easily install your own shading if necessary.

You also need to make sure your greenhouse is quite easily accessible. Consider that greenhouses do need a certain level of attention, so please do yourself a huge favor and build in an easily accessible location.

A southwest-facing greenhouse can potentially overheat due to the sun having additional time in the afternoon, which happens to be the hottest part of the day. It really does depend on your climate, however, and if it does get frigid, then those extra rays of the sun will always help. However, on average, it is better not to build your passive solar greenhouse in this position. Otherwise, you may be finding yourself overspending on ventilation and shading.

If you happen to have a sloped hillside explicitly facing the south, it is a perfect spot for your greenhouse. The earth that faces the north will act as added protection and insulation, but it does ask for more effort in time and a more complicated process. For example, you will need to build a well-structured north wall that can handle the extra pressure of the downward-facing soil.

Insulation

There is a massive reduction in heating costs and higher efficiency when a greenhouse is adequately insulated. The colder the climate you are in, the more critical it certainly gets by far. Proper insulation will act as a way of saving your plants and cut down on all the energy a person would need to spend trying to maintain a specific temperature.

It would be best if you considered several factors while choosing your style of insulation, such as your location, climate and amount of ventilation provided, etc. You will also need to consider the amount of light transmission, considering that the thicker your polycarbonate, the less light you will receive. There is no use in insulating a greenhouse when you cannot get in the proper light and heat for the plants in the first place. You will also learn how to calculate how much insulation you need and want through R-value.

Ventilation

One of the essential components of a greenhouse's success is ventilation. If a person does not have the proper ventilation, the greenhouses and the plants inside will face a storm of problems. Proper ventilation serves four different primary purposes inside of a greenhouse. It helps if the temperature is regulated. It also assists with giving your plants plenty of fresh air in which they can photosynthesize. Finally, good ventilation prevents pest infestations and will help to encourage pollination, which is crucial inside a greenhouse. If you find that your plants are struggling, the first thing you may need to consider is improving the ventilation in your greenhouse.

Looking at temperature, it may surprise you to know that more plants tend to die due to excess heat inside of a greenhouse rather than the cold. Many plants genuinely are sensitive to heat and could wilt. It is best to place vents throughout the greenhouse considering the greenhouse will better regulate the temperature and allow some heat to escape naturally. If your climate is sweltering, then you should consider using an evaporative cooler alongside an exhaust fan to keep your greenhouse cool in many hot climates.

Fresh air is desperately needed for plants to photosynthesize. Considering they need carbon dioxide for food. If the greenhouse lacks good airflow, your plants may not be able to produce as many sugars for their food. This could result in plants struggling as well as dying, so make sure the plants can breathe.

Ventilation helps with pests. It is an odd realization, but poor ventilation does cause plants to become sick. This means they will become targets or attractions to bugs. So keep those fans spinning.

Lastly, there is pollination to keep in mind. A good wind helps for pollination to occur in nature, making a substitute for it within a greenhouse is essential. Moving air will gently shake the plants that help pollination to occur. This is important for plants such as tomatoes which are known to be self-pollinating. A good rule of thumb to remember is that if you see that your plants are not fruiting, you need to add to the level of airflow within your greenhouse. Gentle airflow will also encourage your plants to grow sturdier root systems and stems. The airflow will overall improve the plants' health.

Temperature Regulation and Climate Control

Considering temperature does play an important role, it is only natural to understand the regulation of temperatures to adapt to a climate. A standard greenhouse does require an excess of heating as well as cooling during the changing of environments. It does make it harder to grow the best, fresh local foods when it is not within its season. The solar greenhouse's every intention is to build an energy-efficient greenhouse that is self-sustainable when it comes to temperature control. There are specific strategies that a person would have to undertake when building the greenhouse. The most popular method solar greenhouses regulate temperature is through thermal mass. Thermal masses are known to be dense materials that have the ability to store a large amount of energy (heat). They are placed in the sun, heating up during the day and slowly releasing it during the night. Water is known to be the oldest and the most common form for this. Generally, there are significant water barrels stacked on the northern side, which helps to make a dramatic reduction in fluctuating temperatures.

However, a new and more practical method has arisen which uses the soil underground. It is a free and valuable resource. The earth can be used for thermal energy as well as act as a method of stabilization for temperatures within a greenhouse. In essence, it works like water but does not take up half the space that water barrels do. It also provides more heat and has a more consistent temperature attached to it. This is typically called a climate battery or a Ground Air Heat Transfer system (GAHT) if one wants to be fancy.

In summary, it heats up during the day as hot air gets pumped to the pipes, which are buried underground as is inevitably transferred to the soil, then in the evening, the cooler, drier air transports the heat back into the greenhouse. This is the basic idea of a climate battery and, in reality, far more practical and cheaper than water. The climate battery, along with other forms of thermal mass, will be discussed later in this book.

Now that you understand the different steps and elements to build a successful solar power greenhouse, one can only wonder what steps a person should take to start. This is the beginning of a fantastic journey for you, as well as incredibly rewarding. Now that you have some of the foundational knowledge, it is time to expand it further. You will be exposed to various options and ideas to follow through on, and don't be afraid of the variety. The more variety you have, the better you can choose and build a perfectly tailored greenhouse to your environment, space, and budget.

Chapter 2:
Before You Begin

You are excited to get started. Who wouldn't be? A project this size with enormous potential will have anyone itching to start. Yet, a person needs to be prepared. Planning and preparation are critical, after all. Without them, you are destined to fail or build yourself a poor-quality greenhouse anyhow. So here are a few things you need to consider even before you start to develop your passive solar greenhouse.

Location

As mentioned before, location is essential. Next, you need to consider the orientation of the greenhouse. Consider this, your passive solar greenhouse, in all intents and purposes, is a solar collector in order to encourage plants to thrive in the heat and photosynthesis. The ideal orientation for a greenhouse is to be -15 degrees to the east or south. This applies when you are in the Northern hemisphere. The opposite applies to those who are in the southern hemisphere. This helps to optimize the amount of morning light it receives as well as the heat when the greenhouse is at its coldest.

However, if you have limited options, you can still orient it about 45 degrees off south and still get a great result. In order to fully calculate this, consider using a solar pathfinder. It really doesn't take any batteries and is a great tool to assess and understand the solar resource throughout the entirety of the year. You can also use a solar pathfinder app on both Android or iOS if you would prefer a digital option. Make sure when choosing the site that there is not an excess of shading caused by buildings or trees. A solar greenhouse tends to need as much sun as possible.

Another issue may arise that you cannot build a greenhouse that faces south wholly. However, making it to face southwest (although not entirely recommended) or southeast would still be doable. It is preferable to build it southeast because it helps to heat up the greenhouse faster as the morning sunrises. Moments before dawn are always the coldest, which can certainly assist and help with plants waking up early in the morning.

Climate

Cold Climate

You need to think logically and assess the climate you are in. Is it ordinarily cold weather that occasionally warms up in the summer? Is it blistering hot with a heated winter? Or is it both? Do your research to find out about the climate in which the plants you intend to grow normally thrive. This will all play a role in the insulation and design of your greenhouse. For example, different plants thrive better in the cold, whereas others prefer heat. They all are different and unique in their particular way, and you do need to remember this. Although your greenhouse can practically host any plant depending on how you build it, it might not cover the entire variety that you would want to plant. Instead, set it in different categories, where the maximum of plants that suit a similar environment are the focus in your greenhouse.

You can consider using a USDA tool online to figure out the minimum and maximum temperatures in the area you currently live in. Then, search the temperatures from the climate you would like to mimic the zones you live in, specifically the common plants you are interested in. Even if they are plants around your area, then you can focus on the season in which it grows and flourishes.

Furthermore, there is a tool online you can use to find the best plants for each of the USDA zones, which you can easily find online or by asking plant shops.

Figuring all these out is vital for later calculations that will need to be made. Figuring out your climate is a practical step for working out your ventilation and insulation.

Budget

If you can't afford the cost, unfortunately, it can't be built. Therefore, it is generally a good idea to budget and prepare yourself for rough estimates about the design, materials, and other elements that come inside your greenhouse. On the other hand, it is never a good idea to walk in and purchase items blindly, only to be baffled at the massive bill that comes your way. So, here are some questions to ask yourself:

- What is the amount you are looking to spend?

- And what are the average costs of all the equipment?

- Are there items I would like to save up for?

- Are there tools I can purchase and attach later?

- When does quality over quantity truly matter?

Local Regulation

It is all good and well to build a greenhouse until you are fined and forced to take it down due to a lack of a permit. There are bound to be greenhouse building regulations, and each one would vary from area to area. This is all to make sure the buildings are safe and suited for the environment. So, what are the regulations in your specific location? Do you need zoning or a building permit? It all depends on where you live. However, it should not be too exceedingly challenging to gain a license for a greenhouse, considering its practical nature.

There are two types of permits you need to consider when building a greenhouse. They are known as zoning and building permits.

Zoning permits are found through the local zoning department to see precisely what is required. They regulate where precisely the location of the greenhouse is allowed on the property. It usually means there will be specified plotlines in which you are permitted to build. Whether it is by the side, end, or front is all determined by your community regulations. It also may regulate the number of accessories that you are allowed on your property. Items, such as sheds or other forms of outbuildings, could be considered accessories as well as the size of your building. Specifically sized greenhouses might not even need a zoning permit, but it is all best to do your research and find that out at your local department. Staying both eco-friendly and legal within the laws of your area.

County building departments issue building permits. There are structural codes given to have a peek at both the integrity of the structure and the physical appearance. If you live in a rural area, there is usually no need for permits to build accessory buildings, but most urban areas have at least some requirements. Either way, play it safe and find out. No harm is done by doing a little extra research before starting on a big project like this, especially if the consequences are quite significant.

The building codes typically tackle structural integrity issues and deal with potential weather problems such as wind or snow, depending on the location of your area. Unfortunately, attaching your greenhouse will also be likely to require a permit, just because they are indeed considered to be an addition to your home.

Usually, building codes deal with attached greenhouses in quite a similar fashion as a sunroom. In addition, there are codes to deal with the appearance of the building, which will be different for each community. Some have high levels of aesthetics, while others might be more lenient. However, it is uncommon for communities to disapprove of greenhouses. On the contrary, they usually are welcomed with open arms and encouraged from time to time. You might even find your neighbors coming in asking for tips at the end of the day.

You can also consider getting the help of experienced and local greenhouse manufacturers who are all too aware of the regulation process. They could even help you apply for specific variances and assist you with discussing your plans to groups such as the homeowner's association, as it is their job to stay up to date. They are likely far more aware of the rules than the average communities surrounding them. Even if you are building your greenhouse and not hiring them, what harm is there to find your own information from them?

Common Mistakes to Avoid

A big part of the preparation is to ensure any and all mistakes are avoided when building a passive solar greenhouse. Being aware of the common mistakes people make from the start would certainly help your preparation. Considering many greenhouses have been built over the years, people have made a lot of mistakes.

Humidity

Firstly, be aware of humidity in your greenhouse. Too much humidity will allow mold spores and diseases to grow crazy and fester in your greenhouse. On the other hand, a certain amount of humidity is to be expected. Otherwise, your plants are bound to die of thirst. Therefore it is best to do your research on the plants you want, grouping them according to their humidity needs. It's even better if perhaps you can grow them at the same time. This, however, entirely depends on the amount of space you have in your greenhouse. A good and common way to add to the humidity is through misting, which will be discussed a little later in the book.

Shade

As much as a solar greenhouse is built to soak in the sun, certain plants still need shade, even if it is in the middle of winter! It is wise to consider getting a few greenhouse covers to help shade plants. This is especially helpful in the heat of the day when certain plants need a little fewer rays and a little more darkness. Otherwise, your plants could die from overexposure. It does depend entirely on the plant, as some are designed for as much sun as possible, whereas others may even require shade full time (which means rather grow it in your house if need be). In a greenhouse, plants certainly should be able to survive on a certain amount of exposure to the sun.

There are various shading materials you can get in DIY stores, even online, if need be. You can decide to pull them over the roof and set up an automated system. Or you can opt for the cheaper version and aim for something manual.

Heating

Heating is important and will be covered in-depth later in this book. Consider how the temperature drops at night and how different it is from the day. These fluctuations can damage plants. Frost is a deadly and formidable winter foe that destroys plants literally overnight. It is not recommended for you to use an average house heater for the greenhouse. Quite a few people have done this, and as convenient as it may seem, placing a heater inside your greenhouse is like placing a heater outside. It is just not made for the humidity nor the environment. It is best to use heaters specifically designed for the greenhouse itself or opt for the passive heating methods for a solar passive greenhouse. That is entirely up to you.

Plant Choice

A lot of mistakes are made in the choice of plants. Considering they are the very reason you want to build a greenhouse, it is important to grow the right plants as well. This doesn't mean you are limited, but rather that you need to plan ahead in order to design your greenhouse for the plants you desire. It's good to compile a list of plants you would like to grow and then consider the amount of space, height, and even soil. Some plants are inconsiderate of other plants and may grow too tall (overshadowing other smaller plants) or even aggressively taking over. Believe it or not, some plants do have turf wars. They may be very slow turf wars, but regardless some plants are more aggressive than others, and it is best to be aware of plant behaviors. If other plants grow to the point that they come into contact with the greenhouse covering, they themselves could become root causes for disease, mildew, and even mold growth! Picking your plant is not that much different from picking a pet, after all, it may seem.

Soil Choice

Soil is another common mistake made where people opt to fill their containers with garden soil. Yet this is likely to turn out into a major disaster. Soil normally tends to get compacted, in easier terms, "squished," where the bottom of the container has all the water, and the top is dry. They are not designed to be in pots, after all.

You should rather consider using potting soils and steer clear from garden soils. This makes all the difference in the world. Make sure not to mix them up either, as the temptation may be there to mix cheaper soil with more costly ones to spread them out further. There is a popular practice to grow your plants in something called peat moss or coir. Coir is also known as coconut fiber.

Wrong Fertilizer

As much as people may grab a random bag of fertilizer for their plants, research has to be done even when it comes to these kinds of things. Plants are much like pets in which they have certain requirements in order to survive. However, unlike certain pets, plants can actually be more finicky and may even need something different than your standard one size fits all kind of fertilizer. Much like anything else in life, there is no magical singular formula or soil for all the plants in the world.

So again, grouping your plants to have similar water, fertilizer and shade will save you a lot of trouble, effort, and time. You can even consider adding a certain marker system as an indicator for your plant's requirements, etc. You can add markers for water and stickers, perhaps even for fertilizer, allowing you to have a greater understanding of your plants' needs without having to google it all the time.

A lot of these mistakes may seem obvious, yet when the time comes to build a greenhouse, you may be surprised how often it happens. So take your time in your planning and preparation, as well as learning about the various elements of a successful passive solar greenhouse.

Best Tips Before Building Your Greenhouse

Before building a greenhouse, there are few things to keep in mind. This is to help your preparation and success in the long run. First, you need to have a full understanding of the reasons why you want to build one. Most people tend to have a greenhouse because gardening is amongst the top hobbies in the world. Because building your greenhouse will take time, patience, and maintenance, it is best to make sure you want to build a greenhouse and care for it. It is a commitment you have to make. Here are most of the popular reasons, and make sure it is important enough for you to keep going.

Having a greenhouse allows you to plant all season. Therefore, there is no concern about planting vegetables in the winter, as you are practically in the perfect environment to grow everything.

You do end up saving money, cutting out the costs of plants, lawns, and seeds for the spring season. You will have the ability to grow your own seeds as well as give them away to friends and family. You are also using the space around you for a reason. If you build a large enough greenhouse, you might not even need a gardening shed, as you can store everything you need alongside growing the plants as well. This brings multipurpose and has you being far more efficient with your space.

The greenhouse will also protect the plants from the weather as well as pest infestations. Pests are a very common problem and amongst the main causes of crop failure. Whether it be caterpillars, spider mites, and even locusts, your conservatories keep your plants healthy and happy.

You also do need to consider the cost. How much are you truly willing to invest in your greenhouse? Considering this is a DIY book, you will be shaving a lot of money from other professionals, but it does mean you will have to gather the materials yourself and budget well. Some costs may end up being more than you realized, and even for that, you do need to be prepared. Always have a little buffer to help for expenditures you may not have seen coming.

When it comes to a DIY solar passive greenhouse, you can use pretreated wood, steel, aluminum, or even old windows to help build a greenhouse frame. Recycling is very much possible, and you can even ask your friends, family, and community if they have any unwanted items to get rid of. You can even consider visiting a recycling center or a flea market to fetch some of the materials.

Keeping Pests Out

Although greenhouses are meant to keep pests out, there are still a few things to keep in mind to prevent pests from slipping in, as this is still a possibility that you sorely want to avoid.

Firstly, after you have built a greenhouse, it is best to inspect the plants you bring in very carefully. Look for any adult insects or even eggs, basically any signs of infestation. If you are suspicious of a certain plant, then consider treating it with pesticide before moving it into your greenhouse.

Secondly, it is best to install a good screen for all the openings you have in your greenhouse. This does include your vents and behind attached fans.

Any screens that have an approximate 1/10 inch should keep out most of those nasty pests.

Thirdly, you really need to consider fitting a heavy-duty plastic floor or making sure the base is properly sealed. This will prevent insects from crawling under the walls.

Lastly, it is recommended to keep the area around your greenhouse completely free of any other plants or debris. It was considered that this could be the very item drawing in the bugs in the first place. So, it is just better to have some gravel or plain ground.

Best Tools for Building a Greenhouse

Much like an artist needs a pencil and a canvas so does a DIY greenhouse need a tool kit of their own. Here are some of the items you will need (apart from the materials mentioned in the book). As someone who is already dabbling in DIY and DIY construction, you should hopefully have some of this equipment.

- Long-nosed pliers
- Nut spinners (size depends on what nuts you do use)
- Safety gloves
- Safety glasses

- Screwdriver

- Retractable knife

- A heavy-duty suction cup (especially if you use glass glazing)

The rest does depend on what you plan to do and build. Normally hammers, shovels, and other common construction equipment may be found necessary. Now, you are not required to purchase all the tools. In fact, you could even ask to borrow them from your neighbors temporarily. Then, all you need to do is make sure you have the tool on the day you actually need it. Otherwise, it can slow down your production.

A lot of these are important when planning your passive solar greenhouse. The last thing you want is to build a successful greenhouse and have it infested with bugs from the very beginning. So spare yourself the pain and trouble by planning just a little ahead.

Preparation is key. Without a plan, you are planning to fail. Therefore, it is best to get things right the first time and spare yourself much grief and costs.

Chapter 3:
The Greenhouse Shell and Foundations

Every house that gets built needs to start somewhere. It would be an incredibly odd sight to see someone building a house roof first, then the walls and windows, and finishing the tiles last. Here you will need to make some critical decisions on the overall shell and design of the greenhouse alongside making wise decisions regarding the foundation of a greenhouse. The foundation plays a role in every structure or building you see. However, depending on your choice can also depend on whether you even have a foundation! Alongside the foundation, you need to work out the greenhouse's shell or framework too.

Attached vs. Detached Greenhouse

You may wonder whether or not a greenhouse should be attached or detached. Here are a few pointers for you to consider when securing a greenhouse.

Greenhouse With an Insulated Wall

If you attach your northern or southern side, it will provide a solid wall that is practically already insulated and adds excellent protection for the greenhouse. It certainly makes it more accessible for yourself if you add it to your house and easier to hook up electrical and water accessories. It can also act as a source of passive heat for your house, especially if it is connected to your house by an opening or a door. This works very well for homes that are already using solar heating for indoor thermal heating. However, in a standard home, a person needs to be cautious with glazing to not make too much heat loss or gain. It is also a stunning addition to your house, primarily if you focus on an aesthetically pleasing design. If you also want to spend a lot of time gardening and tending to your plants, this is also a good idea. Especially in winter, it is pretty horrible having to venture back and forth outside in the cold in comparison to only having to walk in and out of a room in your house.

However, some disadvantages of having it attached are a dense humid environment that could condense on any surface. This means that the side exposed to your greenhouses needs to have the ability to handle humidity. So, make sure you learn how to protect your items from humidity damage. It would be best to make sure that everything is waterproof to a certain degree and won't gain mold or rust, or even rot. This is especially a big concern if the wood is involved. It would help if you made sure the wood is treated with anti-rot and can handle the humidity coming its way.

Building another structure on your home may require you to obtain a permit to alter the already existing system. The rules can be far more strict than simply building an undetached greenhouse, as unfair as that may seem.

If you do want to have the look of an attached greenhouse while avoiding certain building restrictions, you could consider building your greenhouse merely a couple of feet from the main structure and create a false wall between the two of them. This does, however, still require you to check with your county to discover the offset restrictions. You could even consider simply making a small walkway between the greenhouse and the main building if need be. Do your best to find out as much as possible about the regulations to stay legal and out of unnecessary trouble.

Space, Aspect Ratio, and Shape

If it doesn't fit, you can't build it. That may seem obvious, but it is easy to get measurements, plans, and ideas wrong precisely when it comes to fittings like glazing. You really want to make sure you get the aspect ratio right. Details matter in this case. Consider this as the footprint of your greenhouse. In order to maximize your solar gain and minimize the loss of thermal heat, it is generally better to have long, narrow, rectangular buildings. You can alter these slightly to make sure it fits in the size and location you have planned for it. Making your greenhouse rectangular will save you a lot of trouble and make your project a little easier.

The shape of your greenhouse is the 3D plan for the building. There are a wide variety of shapes available, but each and every one of them will have its advantages and drawbacks tacked alongside. Here are some of the basic principles you can use to decide the shape, also called your greenhouse's cross-section.

How high does the greenhouse need to be to grow the plants you want? Some plants are naturally taller than others, like tomatoes in comparison to carrots, for example. Some tomato plants can reach relatively high, whereas an average carrot should have more space in the soil.

Where would the lower and upper vent walls go? This all comes down to airflow, which is covered later.

Are there any height restrictions that you do need to be aware of? For example, if you are a tall person and would like to spend considerable time in the greenhouse, the last thing you want to do is constantly bump your head. Yet if you need to reach the roof for other various reasons, then you may want to make it reachable enough.

Is there any form or function that you would like to add to the greenhouse that may require specific overall shape adjustments? This could be the roof or the wall to which you want to attach your greenhouse too.

And what are the ergonomic requirements which you want in your greenhouse? Suppose you do not know what ergonomics is. In that case, it is known as the art of identifying flaws in the production process to avoid any significant inefficiencies from occurring. Thus, it is paying attention to detail, and this is undoubtedly necessary when building a greenhouse.

The moment you have figured out the aspect ratio (the practical ratio between the height and width of your greenhouse) as well as the cross-section (architectural drawings making it three-dimensional), then you have your overall shell design of your passive solar greenhouse.

Kneewall

Common Example of a Kneewall

So what exactly is a kneewall? What part does it happen to play in a greenhouse? A kneewall is the vertical front wall of the greenhouse that happens to be the support of the lower vent system. It works like a sandwich and is traditionally built like a house wall. It is typically recommended to construct a kneewall as thick as you can manage as well as afford. Kneewalls help by keeping the best forms of insulation inside of the greenhouse. It certainly helps to prevent heat from escaping. It is an essential component that sets explicitly out the height at the front of the greenhouse. It also has vertical space that allows snow to slide off the glazing to prevent too much accumulation.

It may be astounding to know that greenhouses need open front vents, even if it is the middle of winter, especially if it is on a sunny day. A person needs to ensure the vents do not get blocked up by snow. It is also best to build the kneewall about three to four feet high (Avis, 2018b). However, if your environment is prone to a high level of snowfall, you would have to consider making it larger or simply clearing the snow every now and then.

Roof

A roof is an obvious addition to the greenhouse. Yet, there is a little more to it than may initially meet the eye. When it comes to solar greenhouses, science and math are frequently involved in creating a flourishing plant-friendly environment. When it comes to roofs, it is all about the angles... literally! The way the sun hits your greenhouse makes quite a big difference. Most people don't really consider lighting or these aspects. Yet when building a passive solar greenhouse, it should be amongst your primary focus.

Many greenhouse professionals do make claims that the angles of roofs are clear and simple. Yet reality does tend to differ a little bit. So there is a bit more strategy involved, and here are things you really need to consider to get the best angle for your house.

There is a little formula called the angle of incidence. The reason why it is named such, and why it is so important, is because the angle of the glazing actually does affect the amount of light that manages to access the greenhouse. Consider shining a flashlight directly on a straight wall ahead of you. You can clearly see a concentrated amount of light has managed to land on it. The same could be said if you shone the flashlight directly through a window. However, if you were to shine the flashlight at an angled mirror or window, you may notice some of the light bouncing off, and the concentrated amount of light is certainly dimmer. The same can be said for the rays of the sun. If the sun's rays hit a window or glaze directly, one could say it absorbs 90% of the light. This is especially true if the glazing is single pane glass. Considering the sun's rays do hit the earth at an angle, it only makes sense to build the roof at an angle too in order to make it as perpendicular as possible to the light.

However, this is where some misconceptions arise. A common pitch is an idea to create a formula by calculating the earth's latitude and just adding 20 degrees in order to calculate the slant of the roof. This does cause issues, however, considering that you will then have an extremely steep roof that is both impractical and could bring along several problems to sort out. The truth is, even if you make the roof slightly off by almost 45 degrees, it will not affect the light transmission too much. It just mustn't be too shallow; extending beyond 45 degrees perpendicular can cause problems and insufficient light transmission.

So, a good way to calculate your roof angle is by finding out the latitude and adding 20 degrees. This is your optimal angle. Then subtract it by 45 degrees to know how far you can alter it without losing a significant percentage of light. In the end, you can then work between the two numbers to build a roof both optimal for the light and practical for you, especially when it comes to the design. This is a practical and strategic way to approach building your roof. The math is not too complicated either.

Different Types of Foundations

The scariest thing to experience speeding on the highway is the encounter of an obstacle course of little bumps and tiny hills smashing against the tires of your vehicle. This is due to a lack of proper foundation and defeats the entire purpose of the road itself. Foundations for a greenhouse might not go as terribly wrong as foundations laid incorrectly on the road, but just like any building, it should be taken seriously. Unless, of course, your greenhouse is small enough not to have to build a foundation at all. Again this is entirely up to you.

You do need to consider these three factors when laying the foundation of your greenhouse: soil connection, the frost line, and your goals.

A greenhouse should have a connection with the soil. Anyone who has watched two plants growing side by side, one in a pot and one in the free ground, can always see a vast difference, where the one in the free soil flourishes bountifully, and the other has a constant struggle. This is because the roots are very limited in pots, whereas on free soil, the plants stretch out as far and as deep as need be.

In order to avoid troubles in winter, the soil does, for a start, need to be below the known frost line, and lastly, it should not be toxic. You can normally tell if the soil is contaminated by certain indications, such as soil discolorations. If there are particularly strong odors coming from the soil, then you may want to reconsider using it. If you also fail to see a lack of vegetation or plants struggling to grow there, it is a good indicator of whether or not the soil is toxic. You do need to consider the history of the area and the land you are in. If you are close to any mining, agriculture, gas dispensing, or even waste disposal, it could leave room for problems. If push comes to shove, you can have a certified laboratory test it, but that is up to you. You just want to make absolutely sure that the soil you use for your greenhouse is fresh and clean.

You also need to have your soil align with your goals, as not all soil is the same. Just like saltwater fish cannot survive in a lake nor freshwater fish in the ocean, the same can be said for the plants. Certain plants live and thrive in specific soil types, whereas others would simply shrivel up and die. As grim as that sounds, the truth remains very clear that you cannot plan your greenhouse under the belief that all plants will coexist and live peacefully in one place. You can consider grouping different plants together with the different soils, though, as this can open up the option of growing a variety of different plants despite their needs.

Foundation Insulation

The ground is a clever and practical way to start your insulation process. Yet you may be surprised at how many people forget or don't realize that they can use the same soil for the greenhouse to help with the heating. Foundation insulation is standard in greenhouses, but many people have started to adopt it for their own residential houses. So, why not add proper insulation for your greenhouse right underneath you? This will boost your overall insulation as well as cut out any necessary electricity costs. This certainly makes it self-sufficient in the long haul.

By insulating the greenhouse, you couple it with thermal mass underground, which gradually releases its heat in the cool of the day and the evening, thus creating natural insulation and an evening out the temperature swings. Although there are many ways to make insulation, it is indeed best to focus on insulating underground. First, you create a soil pocket. This is a way to tap into a gold mine of free heat known as thermal mass (heat stored in the ground below). You may have heard or seen some people bury their greenhouses half underground. This is all to take advantage of the underground heat.

Here are three different types of foundations you can consider building for yourself. The first one directly tackles the issues pertaining to the frost. You can start off by creating shallow foundations and build-in insulated strips that stem along the wall. This does allow plants to have the freedom of expanding their roots while avoiding frost. However, this does place a limitation on the plants you can grow as some need deeper foundations depending on their root type.

You could consider the exact opposite and go for deep foundations where the plants can grow and thrive, and you do have fewer limitations. However, you will practically have to invest in digging deeper, laying down concrete insulated walls, and then only filling up with soil. This does solve the problems you may come across regarding frost, but it does mean you will have to budget accordingly. It will also take a little more time as the concrete will need time to cure.

Another option is to consider shooting for the rubble trench foundation. This is cheaper than the option above yet has been known to last long as well as work against the frost. However, this is not a vastly popular method, and many people are not actually aware of this type of foundation. So, if you intend on hiring someone to build a greenhouse for you, make sure they brush up on the necessary steps in order to create this successfully. The most significant benefit of this form is that little to practically no concrete is actually needed.

However, this may prod you to ask, is an insulated foundation really necessary? Well, truthfully, no. A person can make a passive solar greenhouse without it, but much like there are safety bars on the stairs and pipes for water in houses, it sure helps. Greenhouse foundations can lose approximately 15% of their heat just through the ground (Greenhouse Emporium, 2019). Therefore, in order to help with protecting your plant's roots and adding to your success with your greenhouse, you need to consider insulating it, especially if you want to avoid having to add any electrical assistance to the heating of your greenhouse as far as humanly possible.

You might wonder what a frost line is and how to know how deep to dig. A frost line is considered to be the depth where the ground happens to freeze in the winter. This means the soil on the very surface tends to freeze. However, the deeper you dig, the warmer it gets (due to natural thermal mass) to the point that the soil cannot freeze. This is important to know in a greenhouse, assuming you do not want your plant's roots to freeze and die. Therefore, it makes logical sense to dig below the frost line in order to prevent this from occurring.

A good tip is to consider waiting before digging the foundation if you are currently in the winter. Then, when summer arrives, the ground will be adequately thawed and just make your life overall easier when you are building and digging.

The best way to figure out your specific frost line is by checking out a frost line map. Much like figuring out the latitude and the angle you should build your greenhouse, there are maps to help you figure out the frost line. This does make the work infinitely more manageable as you do not have to be left at the mercy of trying to figure it out yourself. If you want better accuracy, you can check out your frost line using the National Weather Service's map or checking out your zip code.

Also, it is best to avoid any potential water pipes. If you are digging below the frost line, you will actually be reaching low enough actually to damage the water pipes. If you know the layout of your house, be sure not to dig your foundation right where the pipes are. If you are uncertain, then practice extra caution. Of course, a person wants to build their own passive solar greenhouse to save money and be self-sufficient inevitably, but it is best to play safe and avoid a visit from the local plumber as well.

All you really need to dig is a shovel, but you might want to have a pry bar handy if you happen to have large rocks in your area. Unfortunately, you may only discover this after you actually start digging. The fastest way to dig that will save both time and money is renting a handheld drill. You can even consider a Power Take-Off (PTO) tractor (in order to use more power to dig hard soil), and renting makes it significantly cheaper. You are making your life easier in the first steps of building the greenhouse, as it is potentially one of the longest and hardest steps when first starting off your greenhouse.

You will be learning about insulation a little more in-depth later in the next chapter. However, it is best now to understand the importance that a foundation holds. It is not merely to keep a building firm, steady, and upright (which is practically very important). Still, the insulation will help your passive solar greenhouse's journey to become self-sufficient. It isn't that difficult to lay yourself an insulated underground and save you a lot on the electricity bill in the long run and prevent death by frost for many of your plants.

If you happen to build a small passive greenhouse, then you could decide not to have a foundation at all. This is the fastest and most affordable option, but again, it is up to you. On the other hand, suppose you would like to have space and insulation, then a foundation is highly recommended. It all depends on your plans, budget, and goals for your solar passive greenhouse.

Chapter 4:
Insulation and Glazing

Having covered the insulation on the floor, a person can't help but wonder what other steps are to insulate the rest of the greenhouse. Avoiding heat loss is essential, especially in winter. You could wash a couple of weeks' worth of work down the drain just because of one extra frosty day and terrible insulation. This happens so quickly and so easily, so it is best to practice caution and good preparation.

Insulation is crucial for a passive solar greenhouse. You are considering that one actually wants to step away from using electricity, rather than relying on purely natural resources and clever sciences to make it practically self-function. Therefore you want to build smart. After all, work smart, not hard. It also means that you will be having a little bit of mercy on your electricity bill. You will find yourself and anyone else living with you thanking you.

Understanding R-Value

The first thing you need to understand about insulation is R-value. There is a lot of fuss going around about this, and you should especially pay attention to it. So what is R-value? This usually is a form or indication of the thermal resistance that is contained in certain materials. It gages how much an item can lose heat. Anyone who has gone down a metal slide would clearly remember not to wear shorts in the hot summer sun. The same could be said for a metal bench in winter. As quickly as it gains heat, it loses it. This has to be considered when you are building something to store heat and have it be released slowly, like a slow cooker.

R-value works in which the higher the R-value is, the better it is at keeping in the heat. This is very positive in regards to insulating your greenhouse. The thicker the materials are, the more effective they can be to put it as simply as possible. However, materials should also be low thermal conductivity. Otherwise, it loses heat just as quickly as it picks it up (like the example of metal chairs and swings). Or you learn to insulate those items to benefit from the quick transmission without the immediate loss.

So, you can consider R-value to be the key that measures the amount of heat your greenhouse needs and plays a role in the choice of your material. It is a handy tool to work on proper insulation, allowing your greenhouse to function optimally. It is known as the universal metric. You can consider using a formula such as:

Heat Loss = (1/R-value)(surface area)((ΔT) :(Storey, 2017)

There are certain ideas that clever spending on insulating surfaces that have low R-value will get you so much further than investing in items such as highly insulated walls. It is best to focus on the glazing materials, making sure it does have a good R-value.

Why should a person focus on glazing? Glazing is normally transparent or translucent material installed in a greenhouse in order to light in. If you have ever worn a hat on a cold misty day, then take it off. You immediately feel colder. This is because temperature escapes from your ears more than your arms at times. The same can be said for the glazing of a greenhouse. You can wrap it up as tightly as you want to around the rest of the house. However, if you forget the glazing, you will shoot yourself in the foot. Do keep in mind this is all in reference if you were in the Northern Hemisphere. If you are in the Southern hemisphere, then your solid insulated wall would have to be on the south side.

Your north, south, and west walls are also crucial to keep in mind while insulating, considering your passive solar greenhouse doesn't only focus on taking in the sun's energy but also storing it for the colder days and evenings.

The most common reason people fail with the construction of the greenhouse is due to the fact that they design it to capture heat perfectly. However, it slips out of the house as soon as the temperature does drop. Therefore, you need to add insulation on every part of the house that does not play a role in collecting heat and light. This means that you must entirely wrap your north wall in insulation and the east and west sidewalls, considering these sidewalls only get a minor amount of sunlight. Therefore they tend to be more guilty of losing heat than gaining it.

To get a good idea of how much insulation you need, observe other greenhouses if you can. But, again, keep in mind it really does depend on your climate and where you live. If you have rather extreme amounts of heat, you may slacken more on the insulation and focus on ventilation. Still, if you live in an area of cold and frequent winter snow, then you should consider giving your greenhouse the insulation blanket it deserves to keep your plants cozy. If you would like some additional advice about building your area, then consider contacting a nearby greenhouse designer. They can give you information about the climate's analysis, suggestions, and tips to get you started.

The best way to approach insulation is by calculating how much R-value you need. There is something known as interest diminishing return. It means that you can insulate as much as you want, but potentially some of that insulation will be rendered ineffective and take a bite out of your wallet. In practical terms, a person can play it easy and insulate everything they deem necessary, but in the end, it is like adding chocolate flakes to a chocolate bar; it just doesn't do much. So, for someone on a tight budget, here are a few things you can understand when working out the insulation you truly need.

According to Avis (2018c), you can calculate that approximately 58% of your heat is lost through the glazing. Another 11%, 15%, 10%, and 6% are lost through the footing, walls, and roof. So when you double the R-value in the walls, it might only be effective up to about 6%, which means it truly doesn't help as much as you would like it to.

It is commonly known that most heat loss occurs at night via glazing. So, a practical idea is applying a thermal curtain during the night for the glazing, dramatically cutting out heat loss to an estimated amount of 25%. Furthermore, it only costs a fraction of the amount when doubling the insulation on the rest of the walls. Again, however, depending on your climate, you need to cover the general basis and recommendations. Your climate plays a huge role in how you will be building your passive solar greenhouse. The thermal blind is not the only trick you can apply, however. You can also consider screens to trap the heat during the day, but your budget limitations may determine what you can get.

One of the cheapest methods of insulating your plants during the evening is by placing a layer of cover fabric directly over the plants. You can use two or even three layers, depending on how cold it gets. However, to prevent squashing, make sure you suspend the fabrics on hoops or canes. However, although this is the cheapest, it does require the most manual labor.

When you use thermal screens and blinds, these reduce the work as they are transparent, allowing the sun access during the day while cloaking and preventing heat from escaping at night. It would be best if you considered all these aspects, as well as whether or not the size of your greenhouse makes these ideas more feasible or not.

If it is exceptionally cold, then you might have to consider a greenhouse heater. This is not vastly expensive and a great solution, especially if the rest of your insulation is actually well built.

Taking a Deeper Look at Glazing

Glazing materials are equally important when it comes to insulation. As you are now aware, the glazing lets most of the heat escape, but it is as important in capturing it. If the plants do not get enough light, they will not flourish. They could potentially die. Glazing is important, but it has its fair share of downfalls.

Most people find polycarbonate to be the go-to choice, but you can consider going for a double-wall polycarbonate, which is by far cheaper and a good alternative to consider if your budget is tight. To make sure you do choose the correct material, you have to keep a couple of things in mind. First, you do want glazing with the highest potential R-value. However, it still needs to have the ability to let in light by 70% or, better yet, higher. So if you happen to have a high R-value glazing material at hand, but it transmits 60% or lower, then you really shouldn't consider it.

It would be best if you also made sure the glazing is strong enough to withstand the beatings your weather and climate can give. If you are in an area of heavy snowfall, make sure you can hold the load.

If you have a lot of wind, make sure it can withstand those beatings too. Nothing will ruin your project faster than the reality that your glazing gets ripped off and your plants are destroyed.

It would help if you also keep your costs in mind. Buying the cheapest glazing material might turn out more expensive in the long run if it is in constant need of repairing or replacing. This is often where the practical mindset of quality over quantity does trump this situation. You need to remember the amount of light the glazing can transmit, as that is the entire role of your glazing.

Now there is no magical fixed formula in working out the exact right amount of light transmission you need. It all does depend on the area you live in and whether there is a lot of shade surrounding your place. When you are in a really sunny climate, you can go for stronger glazing that transmits less light, but you may need more light transmission in the shadier areas. However, keep in mind the amount of light your glazing can transmit and the strength of the material work hand in hand. The denser forms of glazing tend to transmit less light, whereas the lighter material does transmit more.

It is always ideal for getting your material with a warranty, especially in regards to hail or accidental damage. This can save you a lot of sweat and tears should accidents occur.

There is also a difference between transparent and translucent material. For example, a mirror is known to be completely transparent, and you have no trouble looking through it. However, the glazing that is made of plastic is translucent, which means it is far harder to diffuse the light and isn't always necessarily see-through. It is known that translucent materials are, in general, better for growing plants, and it merely cuts out the nicer view you may receive from a transparent material.

Common Materials

Polycarbonate

Greenhouse Glazing Materials

You have probably heard of polycarbonate as it is the most popular material used to install glazing. It has multiple benefits, namely that it can withstand harsh weather well, is pretty hail resistant, and helps with insulation. It is also exceptionally lightweight and not such a massive burden to install. You can use it to seal the greenhouse professionally and can look quite aesthetically pleasing.

However, it has grown a reputation of going yellow due to all the exposure it may receive from the sun, but recently this drawback has been reduced. Polycarbonate can generally last a person for about ten to twenty years and is slightly more expensive than polyethylene film.

To top it all off, you can receive this form of glazing in a variety of layers depending on what suits your climate best. For example, you can get a standard double layer known to be about eight millimeters thick, or rather shoot for the five-layer, which is 32 millimeters and contains the R-value of 5.6. If they are both a little to the extreme, you can settle for a triple layer that is 16 millimeters and has an R-value of 2.4 (Ceres Greenhouse Solutions, 2017).

The most popular polycarbonate is one that tends to contain one or two layers. They are better on the budget but have fewer insulating aspects to them. This does decrease the efficiency of your passive solar greenhouse, and depending on your environment, you may have to opt for the higher insulating level to avoid spending any extra costs for electrical healing (as the whole point is to make the greenhouse passive and self-sufficient).

Polycarbonates tend to be built with certain air pockets. This creates multi-hollow walls. The air inside of these empty spaces helps to create a higher insulation factor. It is commonly called twin-walled panels and is quite common to use for greenhouses. Some even build triple-walled sheeting to add to the insulation. This is specifically if you are in a colder climate and could use all the help you can get, considering triple-walled sheeting has superior strength and an excellent form of heat retention. There are also thin-walled panels that do tend to offer benefits such as durability, decent insulating values, and light diffusion. You need to choose the layer and method depending on what would work best in your environment.

Tips for Installing Polycarbonate

When installing polycarbonate, there are a couple of things to take into consideration. First, improper installation can result in many drawbacks and reduce the lifespan of your glazing. Yet, they are easily avoidable.

Firstly, discoloration actually only occurs when the polycarbonate is installed upside down. This is because it is designed to have only one side that has a UV protection layer. If it is lying on the wrong side, it will turn yellow because the UV protection is on the wrong side, and the glazing will get damaged. Typically when the polycarbonate sheets are delivered, they have protective films with the correct labeling. It is best to keep the labeling on until after installation to prevent this mistake from occurring.

If moisture, dust, or debris enters the flutes, it is a guarantee that they will never look as nice as they did before. Unless, of course, you decide to blow out each and every flute, which is a painful chore and highly unlikely to happen. This is why you should store your polycarbonate in a nice dry place standing upward. Do not allow anyone to walk on it and seal off the open flutes with vent tape once you have had it installed.

The main concern for most people is leakage. Unfortunately, several mistakes allow this to happen and should be avoided. First, your roof does need to be on a slope of at least 10% in order to make sure all the water is moving. Second, do not allow any seams to run perpendicular to your plants, and make sure that any drill holes are larger than the screws, which will be acting as a sealant. This will give space for the contraction and expansion that may occur with the weather.

Acrylic

Acrylic is not like paints but rather a glazing that shares many similar aspects to polycarbonate. It is cheaper on the wallet and has common trade names, such as "Plexiglas." It comes in the same multi-walled form as its neighbor, and it's an excellent choice for applying it to your greenhouse roof and walls. This form of glazing can also be curved but has less resistance to impact than polycarbonate. It is more likely to shatter under heavy pressure, but it is still quite a strong material. Generally, if you have to decide between acrylic or polycarbonate, do what might turn out to be cheaper in your area. The odds of polycarbonate being more widely available is likely, but if you find acrylic to be the lower price, don't be too scared to use this form of glazing instead.

Created through shards of glass fiber embedded inside a form of plastic resin, it is commonly used for sports helmets and storage tanks. They have a wide variety of translucency and can most certainly be used to glaze your greenhouse. However, do keep in mind the level of light transmission is commonly lower, and it can be flammable, just like having a thatched roof. If you are in an area that struggles with fire occasionally or frequent lightning strikes, then you may have to reconsider. The reality is that most fiberglass greenhouses have indeed been replaced by polycarbonate, so although it is an option, opt for polycarbonate if you can.

ETFE

Ethylene tetrafluoroethylene (ETFE) is a new material that has many shared benefits of polycarbonate. It has good insulation levels as well as light transmission, and it is lightweight. It is known to have thicker material and can be curved if need be. It also has a longer lifespan and is resistant to hail. However, there are very few suppliers in regards to this material, and you should reconsider if you ever need to replace your glazing but just can't seem to find the stock again.

Other forms of glazing are known as film plastic that you can consider for glazing your solar-powered greenhouse. They are known to be low-cost, so if you have a lower budget, this might be what you can consider.

Polyethylene

This is a very popular, inexpensive material, but it does bring some disadvantages alongside it. It is not as long-lasting as polycarbonate and can easily suffer from the sun, snow, or wind. So, you might want to think things through if you tend to live in a harsher climate environment. It normally may only last you two to four years if it is in a very harsh climate. It has very little to almost no insulation, but it does provide a certain element of protection for your plants. It is best to use two layers and create an air gap in between to rectify this issue and create a certain amount of insulation. You could also use row covers as an alternative. In summary, this form of material is best used in climates known to be gentler. You will be doing yourself a huge disservice using this material when you are in an extremely cold and harsh environment.

Solawrap

Another option is using Solawrap. This is a higher quality of glazing you can use. It does have an average R-value of about 1.7 per inch of the material. However, in comparison to polycarbonate, it still contains lower levels of insulation. It is best for moderate environments and can last a little longer than its neighbor polyethylene. You can use this for curved greenhouses as well.

Glass

Glass brings its own fair share of advantages and cons as it is a different material in comparison to plastic. If you want to shoot something like this, you need to be aware that it is transparent rather than translucent. This does mean more light can enter and adds to the beautiful aesthetic of the greenhouse. It does have a variety of insulation ratings. Some can have higher R-values and are sealed very well, and are less likely to expand. This prevents any potential of air leaks which does have the habit of reducing the efficiency of insulation of the greenhouse. Glass glazings are also relatively affordable. They aren't cheap but still relatively moderate compared to other glazing materials you may have come across.

However, glass is heavy and can make installation a lot more complicated and difficult than other plastics. In addition, it does mean your overall framing will have to be boosted in order to support the weight of the glass, which may add to the additional costs.

Glass is by far more fragile than the other options listed and can, unfortunately, break with hail damage or heavy objects that happen to fall. This does add a level of impracticality when using them as roofs. In addition, you have to make sure the glass is tempered if your greenhouse does happen to require a building permit, which can make the glass far more expensive than you may have planned.

Tips on Installing a Glass Glazing

Rather focus on using glass strategically, such as for windows and perhaps the vertical applications whereas using stronger plastic materials for the roof instead.

A good safety tip is not to install annealed glass because if it breaks, the glass shatters, creating long and sharp shards. Stepping or being under it when the breaking occurs can really cause a lot of injuries.

That is why it is best to have tempered glass, which, if it breaks, does so in very small square pieces. This minimizes the risk of injury to a significant effect.

Focusing on Insulation

In reality, glass can provide the highest solar light levels but still is not the best insulator, as it allows a lot of heat to escape during cooler temperatures. It is better to use glass that is multi-pane. However, this can turn out to be quite costly, and you may even have to consider custom ordering it for your specific sized greenhouse. This does mean that if it were to break, it might take a while longer to replace as well as be far more expensive,

If you really want to focus on insulation for your glazing at a more affordable price, then consider the twin-wall polycarbonate. It is easier to cut yourself and certainly has a higher R-value level compared to the glass. In addition, you do not necessarily have to stress having a reinforced frame due to its weight as it is lighter.

All in all, do consider getting curtains for your glazing as it does help to insulate during the evenings. If you have the budget, you can even focus on having automatically controlled ones, sparing you the pain of having to open and close them every day.

However, to make your solar passive greenhouse truly strategic, you can focus on balancing your glazing between both glass and plastic to tap into the benefits of both worlds. You can also be smart with the ventilation and the glazing by finding methods of storing the heat rather than pumping it out of the greenhouse during the day.

Focusing on Shading

Although glazing is meant to add light, sometimes a little shade is needed now and then and is a critical component. Especially if you intend to have sun-sensitive plants where they require shade from time to time. Although one of the main goals of the greenhouse is to get as much light in, there is again a flip side to this.

Shade usually is necessary if you are in hot and arid climatic conditions caused by direct sunshine. This commonly results in leaves that are scorched and bring along a host of pests such as red spider mites. Patchy ripening is also a common issue when it comes to too much sunlight. This can typically be the case for tomatoes as well as peppers.

There are three possible ways you can add shade to your greenhouse. First, good ventilation is needed as well as humidity. Then you can focus on shading in order to tone down the environment if need be.

This typically adds to a more jungle-like effect for your plants, allowing many of them to grow without being barbecued during the course of the day. However, shading isn't necessarily complicated or expensive either, and your main goal should be to also reduce the internal temperatures.

You can add external shade netting. This is when you throw a large piece of plastic or hessian over the roof of your passive solar greenhouse. You can simply use clips to keep it in place and ensure the part is large enough to reach the floor.

This will allow you to comfortably secure the ends with bricks and not have it whipping back and forth as the laundry does on a windy day.

You can also consider using shade paint. It usually is quite easy to add to the glass as need be. It usually is quite resistant to a shower but might be a little bit more of a hassle to remove when the season does come to an end.

The last option is to consider internal shade netting. This is when you fix a plastic weave as tightly as possible in the very inside of your greenhouse. This happens to create a great solution without being outside facing the wear and tear of the weather. Again, normal clips used for the inside of frames are a clever and effective way of attaching them.

However, during winter, the shading is not likely to be necessary as you are far likely to be able to control the temperatures through ventilation. Shading tends to be for the extreme heat environments, just like the heaters are intended for the cold. It is an excellent solution for saving your plants and is quite affordable. What you choose, though, does again depend on the size of your greenhouse. If you have a greenhouse tower above you, trying to throw a shade net over it or even painting may just turn out to be very difficult. Instead, opt for the internal shading. However, if the greenhouse is small and space is too limited, then the paint or external shading might just turn out better.

Avoiding Common Glazing Mistakes

Yet again, it is time to learn from the mistakes of others and save yourself a lot of pain, frustrations, and difficulty. Even with glazing, there are quite a few mistakes that can be made and certainly should be avoided in the long run if possible.

Glazing Material

The most common mistake is making the wrong choice for your glazing material. If you choose glass in a severely hot climate, then you most certainly will be letting too much light and heat into your greenhouse. Choosing translucent or transparent glazing is all up to your local weather. It is best to purchase on the recommendations of your local greenhouse builder. There is certainly such a thing as too much light, and you need to consider it. However, if you do struggle with light in the winter, you can consider adding shading for the summer to save yourself some trouble.

Often, if a greenhouse's glazing is not built-in properly, it can bring in a glare. Anyone who has been in an office building or driving a vehicle knows exactly about this dreaded glare. Having to squint at your screen, or even finding the floor too bright, are common issues of glare that can cause eye fatigue and bring in too much light and heat for your greenhouse. Therefore, you have to consider the sun's position when building the structure of your greenhouse to avoid glare.

Glazing Set-Up

Yet overglazing is also a problem. It occurs when you add too much glass and have too little light entering your greenhouse. This creates the exact opposite of the desired effect and can again make it a less efficient environment for your plants to survive and thrive in.

Temperature & Location

You do need to take into consideration your temperature and location. Many of these mistakes are certainly avoidable if you are careful with your planning. However, don't be hasty, and give yourself the time and patience to wrinkle out any concerns and necessities. The moment you have finished building your greenhouse, you will find yourself an expert in many matters, including your local climate. All these things add up to some degree and effect for your greenhouse. As frustrating as it must be to have to work all these matters out, you are doing yourself a huge favor by planning in detail and planning well. Details matter, especially when it comes to glazing.

These matters depend on what you can afford and what benefits you want to take on. Glazing is an important factor in your greenhouse and should not be underestimated.

Chapter 5:
Ventilation

You can consider ventilation to be the flip side of insulation. You cannot have one with the other in a passive solar greenhouse. Because, just as you want to prevent your greenhouse from getting too cold, you also want to prevent it from getting too hot. Yet you don't want the ventilation to backfire against the insulation. They need to work hand in hand to create a passive environment where everything is working together as it should.

Importance of Passive Greenhouses

Consider this: if your greenhouse does not have proper ventilation, you will be opening a doorway of problems flooding your way. Ventilation happens to play four key parts in your greenhouse. First, they help with the regulation of all the temperatures, allowing your plants to get sufficient air and breath. Second, the air allows a plant to photosynthesize properly, which is exactly what you want and prevents the infestation of unwanted pests. Lastly, depending on the plants, it actually helps with self-pollination.

Common Problems of Underventilation

Temperature is important because plants can die from too much heat. Unless your plant is a cactus, it is best to assume they are sensitive and may end up wilt and die. Consider your climate, and if it has the tendency of getting very hot, then you need to focus on the ventilation.

You need to be wise in your decisions of where you build ventilation and how you build them, including the exhaust fans you want to use. The mistake that many people make is ventilating too well. In this event, the greenhouse does not trap the heat for the evening. Alternatively, the other extreme can happen, where it creates an oversized oven, killing the plants. It is great to find a nice balance in between to create for yourself an efficient and thriving greenhouse.

Passive vs. Active Ventilation

There are different forms of ventilation you do need to be aware of. You need to choose based on affordability, practicality, and obviously your own personal preference in what you believe will be best suited for your greenhouse.

Do be aware that even the best-designed greenhouse has the capability of overheating from time to time. This is because the very design of a passive solar greenhouse is to be a solar collector. So, although it is very much needed for the benefit of your plants, it can at times become a little bit like an oven.

You can consider implementing fans, which are known as active forms of ventilation, or try out the passive methods, which are normally solar-powered ventilators and windows that you can open yourself. The goal of ventilation is to give the air a path of least resistance in order to move. The best method to do this is by planting intake vents lower whereas placing the exhaust vents higher (considering the air lower to the ground is cooler whereas heated air tends to lift). This creates a passive method of airflow which is ideal for someone who wants to build a passive solar greenhouse.

If you want to get really accurate and clever, you can place the vents in line with the natural air movements in your local area. For example, if you normally have easterly winds, then it is ideal to place the intake vents to the east of your house and the exhaust on your west, or vice versa if you happen to have more common western wind.

Having control over your ventilation should be your main idea and goal. If it happens to be really cold, then it may not be the best time to expose your greenhouse to the frigid temperatures outside. The idea is to have the ability to have the ventilation at the right time and at the correct temperature. Many people have come up with a variety of solutions, and you can decide what you would like to implement in your greenhouse. There are three main categories under which they fall.

Manual Ventilation

The first one is manual ventilation. This is practically the simplest and easiest method of opening your doors and windows inside of a greenhouse. It may seem to be the cheapest method, but in reality, it may tally up some more costs. Manual ventilation does require everyday attention, much like a pet, and may even need to be opened or closed during certain times of the day. In addition, as the temperature fluctuates, your ventilation needs to change accordingly. This means you will be racking up a lot of trips to your greenhouse, and depending on where your greenhouse is, this could make it even more difficult.

Solar Vents

Your next option is solar vents. These are obviously powered on a solar basis and tend to open and close depending on the temperature inside your greenhouse. In addition, they tend to use wax cylinders, thus cutting off the need to use electricity and still making your greenhouse as passive as possible. However, they have the reputation of being finicky and sometimes require custom openings considering they may not necessarily fit into your precise design. Therefore, it is best to plan your ventilation alongside the structuring and framework of your greenhouse in the first place.

Another issue that may arise is the need to protect your vents from snow, or possibly, extreme winds when they open. If too much snow falls into the vents, it can actually cause a blockage and a breakage. Therefore, it is advised not to build your vents on the roof or any potential spot where snow could accumulate. The same could most certainly be said for the winds where the vents could be accidentally used for a sail and get damaged therein.

Keep in mind that most vents you purchase at the store will not be airtight. Therefore, it is up to you to make sure that the vent you put in is fully and properly sealed before it becomes one of the major heat loss factors in your greenhouse.

Mechanical Ventilation

Another form of ventilation is a mechanical system, which uses fans or other forms of mechanical devices. This allows the greenhouse to create proper circulation as well as a proper form of airflow. The best advantage to this is because you have a very high level of control over the ventilation of the greenhouse. In addition, this form of ventilation does not rely at all on natural elements of the wind or thermal buoyancy. You can also fully automate your greenhouse with this method.

Strategic Ventilation

There are certainly different places you can install your vents that are strategic and work alongside the natural habitat of your environment. Naturally, it would be ideal to have a passive form of ventilation, as it is the cheapest, but this does depend on your climate. Because you will be focusing on the effect of the wind and the buoyancy of temperature in order to create your passive ventilation system, you can take advantage of the wind outside the greenhouse in order to bring in the fresh air to your greenhouse. That is if your local area happens to have a lot of wind. Not every environment will have this advantage.

Example of Passive Ventilation

Thermal buoyancy also works on the reality that hot air rises as the cool air enters. This allows air movement to occur in a more natural way as well.

The best way to fully use this to your advantage is by placing the vents strategically around your greenhouse through roll-upsides, wall vents, and even roof vents. The vents on the walls and the roll-ups tend to allow the air into the greenhouse, whereas the roof vents allow the hot air to exit above.

Keep in mind, this can be strategic, but it can also cause problems if you intend to use the hot air for thermal mass, especially a climate battery. If you are in an area where you do not tend to use a climate battery but would rather focus on ventilation, then, by all means, go ahead. It is just a good rule of thumb to keep in mind when building your passive solar greenhouse.

The one drawback to passive ventilation is the reality that you will not have much if any, control over the ventilation that takes place. You can most certainly feel free to take advantage of the weather, but do not expect a perfect commercial timeline when all you happen to have is passive ventilation. It might end up not being sufficient, which can result in your plants suffering and paying the price.

This is why having an active cooling system is important. Creating an environment where an average wind speed between two or even three miles per hour is ideal and recommended. However, for a passive system, it will rarely reach this goal, and this is why you do want to have an active cooling system specifically designed for your greenhouse.

When it comes to an active cooling system, mechanical tools such as evaporative coolers and fans are required in order to create the necessary and needed movement in the air. Fans are, however, sorely underestimated, but they are very effective as well as efficient. They tend to be overlooked or even forgotten, but any professional greenhouse builder can tell you all the benefits the fans bring to the table. Anyone who has a fan in a hot climate can tell you they bring along their own form of cooling.

It works because the walls pull the air in using a damp pad, which then gets distributed by the fans. As a result, the air is by far cooler and humid than it was outside, allowing for a more amicable environment on a hot summer day.

This does cost more money, however, and a certain amount of electricity too. This is why it may be better to install passive ventilation alongside an active one to work hand in hand and cut any extra costs. The days that work well for your passive system will shave off your electricity bill and still keep the greenhouse going on an efficient basis. It is known as blending your passive as well as your active ventilation together in order to grab the advantages of both, enjoying the benefits of both worlds while cutting down on the cons of others.

How Much Ventilation Is Needed?

Again, considering you are building yourself a custom greenhouse, there is no direct answer to this question. Rather just a few helpful tips and strategies to make sure you adapt it according to how you need it. In order to get a good idea of the number, consider contacting your local greenhouse designer, or you could try using some calculators online. A lot of these problems can truly be solved with a little math which can make things a little easier. Even if you are not a big fan of math, calculators are there for a reason as well.

Here are a few tips to help your journey along. First, be aware that if you use passive vents, the total area in which you can open in the greenhouse should be an estimated 20%-40% (Ceres Greenhouse Solutions, 2015a). Again, this number does depend on your climate. Naturally, if it is colder, it is better to opt for the 20%, whereas if you are in hotter weather, then you could consider the 35% or 40%. You also need to keep in mind the glazing and how much heat is being let into the greenhouse as well. If you happen to have shading, you might actually want to decrease the ventilation if it is quite cool already. All of these are factors you may need to take into consideration. This is why it is recommended time and again to speak to a professional greenhouse builder. Although you are fully capable of building this greenhouse completely on your own, there is no harm in finding out information from someone who builds greenhouses for a living. In fact, it is wise to ask for help every now and then. This gets you quite a couple of steps farther than those who just try to go for it completely on their own.

If you plan to use exhaust fans, then a good rule to keep is allowing the fan to provide a ratio of one to three air exchanges every hour. Even using Ground To Heat Transfer (GAHT) can actually provide a similar system to this, so if you have installed a climate battery, you need to take it into consideration as well. They work partially as exhaust fans too and need to be added to the total amount of exhaust fans you would like to install. Therefore, if you do have a climate battery, it is recommended to then install smaller fans alongside them.

All in all, just like you would like to determine the amount of R-value to put into the greenhouse, it is all about working out the sum total of everything. This is where you might need to experiment with your plans, especially if you would like to combine your passive ventilation with mechanical.

Ventilation Volume Rates During The Seasons

There is normally an accepted rate of ventilation when the summer season heats (Garden & Greenhouse, 2012). This is about one air change per minute. How do people measure this? Well, fans are normally rated through the amount of air volume they actually move. This is usually used in the ratio of cubic feet per minute.

Naturally, it makes sense that you need to work out the total volume of your greenhouse in cubic feet. This is done by multiplying the length and width together alongside the height of your greenhouse.

This will give you the measurements of your greenhouse's volume.

Keep in mind, the greenhouse's roof does happen to come at an angle. Thus your greenhouse is not a perfect rectangle, and it does mess a little with the math. It can make the calculations just a little bit more difficult. If the thought of math is scary, worry not; a degree in geometry is not actually required. Just a little brush up on some math you have learned in school (this is where people who ask where and how they solve X can actually help them until they decide to build something, say a greenhouse on their own). The easiest and simplest approach is by adding the average 10 ft height that is tacked and constant for the average greenhouse.

It may not be as entirely accurate as you had hoped, but it will still do the job. For example, so you know, the length of the greenhouse is about 50 ft, and the width is estimated to be about 20 ft. Then you can add the 10 ft constant height and multiply those numbers together is equal to 50 ft x 20 ft x 10 ft = 10,000 cubic feet (a calculator was used to work this sum out, do not be afraid to use one).

Now that you know your greenhouse is 10,000 cubic feet, then you would want to exchange and install fans that either have a rating of 10,000 cubic feet or get yourself another couple of fans to help the greenhouse out.

When winter comes, ventilation is needed at the minimum and almost never used to help with temperature control. During the fall and spring seasons, the volume requirements are bound to vary. There will be a balance of having to remove excess heat or add humidity, depending on the days. Consider autumn and spring are not as tightly bound to weather patterns as winter and summer are. This is where automated systems are proven to be more effective as they adapt to the day-to-day changes and environment. On a cold day, they focus on insulation, whereas on a hot day, they increase ventilation. It will be tough having to determine every single day yourself what the greenhouse needs to prioritize.

A good tip would be to consider oscillating fans. They are a handy tool used to create uniformity and great air movement. They also have the habit of extending the amicable conditions for longer periods of time. You could also consider using perforated polyethylene tubes to assist in the distribution of fresh air.

It would not be too far-fetched to claim that ventilation plays a role in something as simple as some of the plant functions, such as photosynthesis. It may also play a role in how the plants are pollinated, blooming flowers, and creating idealistic environments for you to grow whatever plants you truly desire. But, of course, it all hangs on the balance of planning ahead, and making sudden quick changes could hinder your success.

Common Questions Asked About Ventilation

As you start working on your greenhouse, you may come across a few questions about ventilation and find yourself a little stuck. Here are the most frequently asked questions about ventilation that should help your journey forward.

First, what does it mean to have a weather station? And why is it a good idea to have one? As well-built and designed as your greenhouse maybe, you do not want to be surprised by the weather. Weather stations are used to collect any and all info on the temperature, humidity, and even solar levels that surround your greenhouse. Some can even go as far as to measure the direction of the rain and the wind. You can install the weather station to work together with any automated systems indoors, which will allow your greenhouse to function with the proper knowledge necessary.

It is easy to underestimate the heat as well as the humidity as it is not something a person can measure with their eyes. You should consider installing a weather station where it is accessible. It does need regular maintenance and cleaning to keep accurate readings. This is especially important if you are surrounded by birdlife and leaves. It is best to purchase a higher quality system that will last you longer, as your data is really only as good as the sensor provided. Additionally, it would be working every day, and anyone knows that in itself is a major factor of wear and tear.

What Exactly Are Greenhouse Roof Vents?

Although it has been discussed, a lot of confusion could still arise about its roles and importance. Roof vents are cooling vents placed on the roof of the greenhouse that can be opened to release warm air. Cooling vents are by far one of the best methods to cool down your greenhouse. This is especially useful if you are in a very hot environment. The roof vents expel the hot air and pull in the cooler air from the ground.

Chapter 6:
Climate Control

Climate control fits the centerpiece of both ventilation and insulation. This is practically the knob you would use to create the reality of a thriving atmosphere for your plants. Having control of your temperature in your passive solar greenhouse is the biggest benefit. This is the fourth element you can implement in order to maximize the heat you gain in the winter and reduce it in the summer.

Understanding Your Climates

There are five main types of climates that exist on this earth. In total, there are many more than just five, but for the purposes of building a greenhouse, these five matter most. In order to plan the best strategy for your greenhouse, it is best to brush up on the climate that you are in and understand how the seasons in your region will go. Now you may have lived there for a few years, but people may actually be surprised how little they truly pay attention to the environment until it avidly affects them.

The climate is known to be the average condition of the weather that remains so over extended periods of time. This is known on average to be about 30 years or more. Even though the weather is altering every now and then, there are certain patterns that still remain the same. For example, winter comes at a certain time, and spring rises up afterward. However, how hot your summers are and how cool your winters tend to be, changes from environment to environment. Some areas are certainly trapped in an eternal winter, such as Antarctica, while other places have an eternal summer, such as Tanzania in Africa.

The closer you are to the equator, the hotter most regions will be. This is because you are getting maximum exposure to the sun's light. Whereas, on the North and South poles, a person gets the least amount of sunlight. This leads to an average of being a couple of days in complete darkness at times, making it a little impractical to build a passive solar greenhouse there. However, these are examples of the most extreme situations, and most people are more exposed to average forms of winter and summer.

Using this information of the different climates, a German scientist, Wladimir Koppen, divided all the different climates of the world into various different categories, these are: tropical, dry, temperate, continental, and polar.

Tropical climates are known for their hot and humid areas and tend to have higher levels of heat along with excess amounts of rain. Building a greenhouse in this environment would certainly mean focusing on ventilation and less intake of light from time to time.

Dry climate zones, as the name implies, are known to be dry due to the rapid evaporation of any moisture. There is also very little rain that occurs and again more excessive heat. Ventilation for a greenhouse in this environment will certainly be crucial.

Temperate climates have the knack of being quite warm in the summer alongside thunderstorms and an average level of humidity. On the other hand, the winters are mild and tend to be less extreme. Again, for a greenhouse, one would add some insulation to help during the winter, but ventilation pulls out again as the first priority.

Continental climates are known for their mildly warm or cool forms of summers, but their winters are very cold. It is common to experience snowstorms and possibly strong winds in this environment. For a passive solar greenhouse, a person would have to focus on excessive light and higher levels of insulation. Ventilation will still be needed, but it is not the highest priority in this climate zone.

And finally, polar climates are known for their frigid, cold environments and are what people would describe as the eternal winter, as in summer, the temperature may not even rise above 10 degrees celsius. To build a greenhouse in this environment will focus heavily on insulation and light transmission with a little bit of ventilation to keep the airflow going. There is not much concern about a greenhouse overheating in this environment as the climate is devoid of most warmth.

Consider visiting the web and finding out exactly what your climate zone is and what your weather patterns are like. It is best to plan what you intend to prioritize before even starting to build your passive solar greenhouse.

Misting: Why You May Need It

It is best to understand that the sun releases infrared light through the greenhouse. A lot of this gets converted into thermal energy, which in turn converts to thermal radiation. The materials you use to build a greenhouse, however, are not able to transmit it, thus trapping it inside. This happens to create the ideal warm and humid environment that plants tend to thrive in. This is practically a nurturing area in which many plants can grow in your greenhouse but may not last a day outside of your greenhouse.

There are multiple greenhouses that close down because of the extreme heat. This occurs when a greenhouse is unable to maintain the passive cooler temperatures, even if they have ventilation. If you are in a climate that has extremely hot summers, then this is exactly why you should consider installing a greenhouse misting.

When installing it, you tend to help your greenhouse fend off certain diseases in plants, boost the growth rate of your plants and germination, and actually could be therapeutic to the plants (in simplest terms, the stress on plants reduces). With a misting system, you are more likely to maintain control of the humidity levels and help to ensure proper plant growth. If the humidity is too high, it can damage plants, but the same can most certainly be said if it is too low. Plants actually tend to stop growing if the level of your humidity drops below 30 degrees. So, when you install a mist system, it tends to be an easy solution to what may seem to be a big problem.

Another cool hack is that you can use greenhouse misting to apply the fertilizers. It basically allows you to spray it on a constant basis, letting the plants absorb it and use it to grow and thrive optimally. Installing it is quite easy and can help you have a level of control over your environment. From the light to the ventilation to the humidity, having control allows you to build the best environment for your specific plants.

Keep in mind that for about every 10 square feet of space in your greenhouse, you need to spend about one or two gallons of water every hour. Then, to work out the total amount of water, you can simply work out the number of nozzles multiplied by the rate of flow in a minute. Then finally, you can take a calculator (if you haven't picked one up already) and multiply that answer by the total minutes a person happens to have in a day. This is about 1440 minutes in a day.

You can additionally install extra devices to help regulate as well as properly keep maintenance over your greenhouse. Even having a timing system should help control both the frequency a well as the length of the sprays that may occur. This means it won't be up to you to spray every five minutes to every hour, but rather just set up an initial system in the first place.

You will need to decide what kind of nozzle you would like for your misting system. It could be brass or stainless steel as they are recommended due to their durability. There are also a few other items you may need to take into consideration. You firstly need to focus on low-pressure systems. When you get yourself medium or even high pressure, it ends up being an extra and unnecessary expense. Focus on getting nozzles that perhaps have 1/2 inch of tubing.

Keep in mind that the smaller the nozzle is, the finer the mist will be. However, the finer the mist, the more likely it will be evaporating directly in the air before it even reaches the soil. This is actually a positive aspect, as you do not necessarily want everything around you to get wet. If you would prefer constantly damp soil, then go for a bigger nozzle. If you do find that everything gets a little too damp, then all you need to do is turn off the system just for a little while to allow things to dry. Considering that you are using the misting system in the summer heat, it is going to dry relatively quickly.

You also want to focus on devices that are actually anti-drip. If your nozzles are misting and you switch them off, then you may find some undesirable results with the dripping. This is why it is infinitely better to install anti-drip devices to prevent drips from occurring.

Do recall that a greenhouse misting system will be operating for hours to days on end. Therefore, make sure you purchase quality, durable materials.

Maximizing Light and Reducing Heat When Necessary

The design of a passive solar greenhouse relies on strategy. A strategy that should be used to fully maximize the light in the winter whereas reducing it in the summer. Again, it does depend on the climate you reside in. Some areas are known to be abundantly colder even in summer, whereas others need more focus on absorbing light even in summer. It is all up to you to determine things with your weather.

Keep in mind that the angle of the sun alters during the four seasons. Anyone who has windows facing the sun can confirm this. For example, during the course of winter, it is quite common that the light of the sun hits at a much lower angle than when it is summer. This obviously regulates the temperature and the seasons. Remember, though, the angles to which the sun strikes the surfaces also change depending on where you stay. These are all strategic calculations you will have to make.

If you have vertical southern surfaces, then you may want to focus on a higher, light-transmittance glazing. The best surface for that, as you may well know, is glass, which soaks in the highest amount of light and heat. However, insulation is sacrificed to a certain degree, but there are strategies you can undertake to combat this too. When you need to prioritize light and heat absorption, some things sometimes need to give way. You can focus on your thermal mass to regulate the heat during the evening and have a great strategic combination of both high-absorbing light and heat while having strong insulating factors with other tools and tricks. It all depends on your priorities, and keep in mind that while you may sacrifice one benefit, there should be another trick you can use to combat and bring some of it back. Again, keep in mind the angles as well. Do not be afraid to revisit a chapter in order to brush up on everything you need to know when designing your greenhouse.

When summertime strikes, you may end up with the exact opposite problem, depending on where you live. On average, most of the climates do give off too much light and certainly do not hold back on the heat. You get extra hours of daylight to top it all off, and you can consider light to be lower in demand for your greenhouse this time of year. This is where you want to focus on glazing that is more translucent and not transparent, such as polycarbonate that has twin layers.

Thermal Mass

As mentioned before, there are several ways you can focus on keeping your passive solar greenhouse cool during the summer and warmer during winter and evenings. There are multiple options available for you, such as concrete, rock, water, or water and glycol, all of which can store quite a large amount of heat in a confined space. There is actually an endless number of elements you can use for thermal mass, and you need to decide on affordability, as well as the level of thermal mass you would like to put in it. In order to help the whole process, you can use a calculator designed to work out the total amount of thermal mass you are recommended to get. It takes into consideration your weak point, AKA your glazing, as well as the material you would very much like to put in (like concrete or cob).

To simplify the idea, it is better to see more thermal mass than less. Again, there comes the point where too much can really inhibit the production space of the greenhouse. It is very much like your insulation and ventilation; you need to discover a fine balance for yourself. Furthermore, the materials that you choose also bring along their own pros and cons. You have to be aware of them, especially if certain materials happen to be freezable while others are non-freezable.

Looking at non-solid materials first, they normally have the capability to freeze. So, for example, if you want to use water as your thermal mass, you have to keep in mind that it can freeze. This makes it a challenge, as the very point of it is to provide heat. However, it is a cheap option, thus holding to its appeal, and is still very capable of holding a high amount of thermal energy.

Using Water Barrels for a Solar Greenhouse

When a passive solar greenhouse is used for yearly plantations, it can go through all the extremes of that climate. The structure itself happens to absorb and collect excessive amounts of heat during the day, allowing a place to overheat quite easily. Yet if not built properly, it can easily lack insulation and freeze during the night. This is why people who own a greenhouse turn to a more stabilized form of maintaining the temperature by focusing on cooling the greenhouse during the day and heating it over the night. These strategies are known to be quite reliable yet costly as well. It is, furthermore, quite a chore to maintain the efforts you put in, and thermal mass is the solution to this problem. Nevertheless, they provide the best passive and natural solution to balance out the temperature spikes that may occur.

Water is the cheapest material and possibly the most popular one that is used for a greenhouse because it can retain the highest level of heat and is quite readily available. Every person would need a proper storage container because anyone could tell you that simply pouring it into the foundational soil of the greenhouse will get you nowhere fast (apart from hiking up your water bill, to say the least). Most people opt to use a storage container, which is quite easy to get a hold of and affordable as well.

The idea would be to stack a couple of large drums containing water into the greenhouse, creating a form of water wall that can be seen as the large thermal battery inside your passive solar greenhouse. One of the major drawbacks is that it can take up a large amount of space, which normally would have been able to be used for growing. So, you need to consider this option for the space you hope to have in your greenhouse. The smaller your greenhouse's natural design is, the more difficult this situation becomes.

If you would like to use a water wall, you will probably have to build a bigger greenhouse in the first place. Water walls tend to be used in greenhouses that are large or even commercial greenhouses. They are structured and designed to give the necessary space. You can consider stacking up the barrels against the insulated wall (whether north or south depending on where you live). Or you could consider using the barrels to actually elevate your plants. There are plenty of ways to use the advantages and bend the rules of your water wall if need be.

A good rule of thumb is to also ensure that your water barrels are in a darker color. Whether you purchase them that way or simply paint them is up to you. Dark colors tend to absorb and contain heat a little better than lighter colors. It's a small but useful detail to consider.

When using water barrels, it is harder to maintain temperature control. This is due to the fact that ventilation fans and heaters have settings to operate at specific temperatures, whereas water can be a little unpredictable from time to time. As much as anyone wishes they can control water, it is best to stick to science. This means water relies heavily on solar energy, and therefore this can become a problem if you suffer from really cloudy and cold weather on a more frequent basis. So, if you need another solution, you can consider using phase change material (PCM). This is a great alternative and will be covered later in this chapter.

Taking a Deeper Look at Your Water Barrels

Water barrels are ideal for someone who has a tight budget and faces severe temperature swings in their environment. It is a sustainable method in comparison to just insulation and ventilation, and it especially fits the theme of having a self-sufficient greenhouse.

However, you need to make sure you install the water wall where it can be exposed to a certain amount of light in the winter and shaded in the summer. This is the ideal scenario but might not necessarily work out as such in your design. You can do this by having a partially insulated roof, and the water barrels are placed on the north side of the wall if you are in the northern hemisphere. If you are in the south, then naturally place the water barrels on your south wall.

In order to find the appropriate amount of insulation to fully understand or figure out when your water wall will have contact with light or shade, you can work out the solar angles. This is based on your location, and you can use a tool such as a sun chart program in order to create for yourself a diagram that plots the pathway of the sun. Then, you can consider using a protractor program and create an estimation of your roof length. It is best to ensure the place you put your wall will be shaded in the hot summer days and have a glimpse of the sun in the winter.

Phase Change Materials

The solid materials, known as phase change materials (PCM), on the other hand, do not have the high level of storage of thermal energy as water does. In fact, they have approximately four times less, but they do not freeze the same way water does and are far easier to set up without the need for further necessary maintenance overtime.

If you do desire to get a little more out of your greenhouse or prevent the need of having to dive in for repairs or replacement on your thermal mass, then you may want to consider phase change materials. PCM are used to absorb the energy of the sun during the day while releasing it at night, similar to water. PCM has the capability of keeping your greenhouse warm during the winter, especially the winter evenings. It is quite easy to add it to a greenhouse, even if it has already been designed and built-in, which allows a little bit more flexibility. For instance, if you do release the water walls that are not working, then switching or even adding phase change material is certainly an option.

How exactly does it work, though? Well, PCM works on the basis of the transference of energy, taking advantage of the natural changes that occur during a day. For example, a certain material changes in phase. It turns from solid into liquid and finally into gas that creates energy. This energy works as molecules that tend to combine and break apart from time to time. During the day, the PCM melts, taking in all the heat that comes through and solidifies at night. While it freezes, it releases the heat in the evening, passively warming up your greenhouse.

It is possible to use water in this form, but in reality, the PCM just works better. It takes in approximately five times the same amount of heat storage in comparison to water. The reason why is because it uses the physics of latent heat.

What is the physics of latent heat? Well, latent heat is known to be energy that has been absorbed and released through the use of a substance. This is when the substance's physical state changes from solid to liquid and gas. For example, when it is melting, the solid or liquid that is freezing is normally called the heat of fusion, and when it turns into a gas, it is known as the heat of evaporation.

A great example to use is that of a pot of water. While it is boiling, it is kept at the temperature of 100 degrees celsius. The temperature will remain so until everything has fully evaporated. This is because the evaporation that occurs is so large that it carries the thermal energy with it, releasing it once it condenses. This is ideal for creating thermal mass inside a solar-powered greenhouse. You will be using materials that change phases during the different temperatures.

So, phase change material, once installed, is practically free throughout the winter. It helps to even out all the swings of temperature evenly and creates an amicable environment for the plants. It is a very efficient energy source to be considered in your budget if you can since it focuses on the yearly aspect of the greenhouse and fewer concerns of it freezing over like water. Phase change materials, on average, have a better reaction to warmer temperatures than water, which freezes at 32 degrees Fahrenheit. However, with phase change material, it tends to be compatible for both hot and cold regions and seasons. All you need to do is tailor it according to the temperatures you are expecting.

Phasing change materials are quite easy to get a hold of, and it doesn't take a licensed person to install them. It tends to come in sheets that are nailed onto a wall for practicality. This reduces the space needed for thermal mass, such as water cans, and can literally be placed on any surface of the greenhouse. You can add as much as you believe is needed for the thermal mass, and it stays far out of your way, which is incredibly convenient if you have a small greenhouse. It is not too far-fetched to say that PCM is desirable for any passive solar greenhouses.

However, if you happen to be in cold and cloudy climates, where you cannot rely as heavily upon the sun, you may want to consider investing in a Ground to Air Heat Transfer or (GAHT). This is used to take advantage of the thermal mass in the underground soil, allowing it to store excess heat in the summer and slowly releasing it in winter. This means it works as an extended battery.

Climate Battery

Climate Battery, known as the GAHT system, is a clever thermal system using a couple of small fans. On an average day, a greenhouse absorbs a lot of heat, which is normally expelled through a ventilator, but this can truly be considered a waste.

However, the climate battery focuses on drawing in any of the excess heat into the soil where it is stored and kept. A way of recycling the daylight heat, so to speak. The moment the greenhouse gets hot enough, there is a thermostat that switches on the pumps, moving the hot air into the soil. The moment the hot air reaches the soil, it is absorbed into the soil, and cooler, drier air tends to come back up into the greenhouse. This practically makes it work as a ventilation system at the same time.

When evening or even winter comes, it works the same way to a certain degree. The fan, this time, draws in the cooler air, picking up the warmth in the soil and bringing the heat back into the passive solar greenhouse. This heat is the excess of what has actually been collected throughout the entirety of summer, not just the entirety of one single day. This makes it far more reliable with unpredictable weather and takes away a certain amount of dependence on the sun the whole time.

The tool kit of a GAHT system merely requires a couple of fans and a clever piping system that leads directly underground. It is taking simple sciences and using them fully to your advantage. Although it does make your greenhouse completely passive, it still saves you a lot of energy and electricity in comparison to other systems out there. Furthermore, some climates are so extreme that expecting your passive solar greenhouse to survive on its own is risky. Sometimes it just needs a small nudge here and there to help it along. Besides, it is still a self-heating system, as your greenhouse merely relies on the heat that has been stored in the soil, collected by the solar energy during the summer anyhow. It can certainly work in severe climates such as heavy snowfall and rain.

Another rule of thumb to remember is that the more humidity is in the air, the higher amounts of energy that can be stored. When the warm air is pumped into the soil, it condenses, which is the form of energy released into the soil. In order to make sure the whole system works properly, you have to make sure you have the correct duct sizes as well as correct sizes for fans. Otherwise, you do not use enough power, and the air does not actually reach the storage space. If this does happen, then you might as well have gone direct electrical heating elements instead. Because then you are practically storing nothing. This is quite a fatal mistake to make for your greenhouse, as by the time anyone might realize it is already winter, and no heat has been stored. So, it is better to ensure everything is done right from the start.

In order to make sure you build it correctly, you may want to use a SHGS design tool, a heavy-duty clamp, which allows a person to choose the diameters of the duct through the size of the fan. It is best to have a speed fan that can vary to improve the overall system. Also, it is best to install it as such so that you can change the fan speed and airflow rate that is optimal for your greenhouse, decreasing and increasing if need be.

Building Your Climate Battery: the Do's and the Don'ts

It is commonly said that it is wise to learn from your mistakes. However, one should call that knowledge and experience. It is wise when you learn from the mistakes of others before making costly ones of your own. So, when building your climate battery, there are a few things you may want to keep in mind, especially when it has cost others quite a penny and even failed in their greenhouse design. The very idea of learning all these tricks is to ensure your success, and what better way than to look at the mistakes commonly made by others and avoid them?

The idea behind a climate battery is simple, yet when it comes to the actual steps to building, it can turn out to be a lot trickier than expected. Here are a few do's and don'ts to keep in mind and elevate your success with this design.

You do need to create a proper plan at first, considering any small mistakes can actually make this design become useless and will frustrate you endlessly if it doesn't work. Most of the pitfalls when it comes to designing these climate batteries are avoidable, and this is where you really do need to pay attention. As mentioned above, one of the most common mistakes made is when the fans are too large or way too small. The way and amount of heat you manage to store all rely on the reality of how well and fast your air moves. You need to make sure that your heating, as well as your cooling capacity, is functioning at an equal rate. You have to make something that is powerful enough to push the airflow down, but if it is too powerful, the heat transfer doesn't occur. Rather, it simply rushes through the pipers and right back out again into the greenhouse, practically making the air go in pointless circles and defeating the entire purpose of the climate battery.

Another common mistake occurs when calculating the tubing diameter. They are designed to be too small or too large and should be calculated with the amount of airflow in them. If the pipe is too small, this will create a certain level of resistance and just a general reduction of heat storage and efficiency. Therefore, it is unlikely your climate battery will perform optimally and again possibly defeat the purpose of your design. If the pipes are too large, however, you end up losing a lot of the heat, thus reducing the heat and again the efficiency of your climate battery.

It is important to know how deep you should dig and place the pipes as well. Normally it is recommended to place the pipes around two to four feet below grade (Ceres Greenhouse Solutions, 2021). This allows the pipe to be deep but remain above the water table in the soil. If it happens to be buried in too shallow of a space, you are likely to lose the total store heat that you can use. It also works as a prevention of creating stable temperatures for the soil.

Furthermore, be aware of making the pipes either too short or way too long. There are multiple ways you can decide to connect as well as lay out your pipes in the soil. You can have it connected in multiple ways or even just have it connected in a single system. That is up to you and your greenhouse design. If the pipes happen to be too short, the time frame in which the hot air is transferred to the soil will not be enough. This will yet again reduce the efficiency of your climate battery. However, if the pipe is too long, the pump will struggle. You will end up reducing the airflow at a significant rate. This means it will store the heat nicely, but when the time comes for the airflow to pump back the heat, it will be sorely lacking.

Another common error you need to look out for is air leaks. This normally comes from improper sealing of pipes and again acts as a reduction of airflow. There is also drainage needed in the pipes in order to prevent or clean out the mold and potential blockages. Considering that it is warm, dark, and humid, it is an ideal breeding ground for mold and could cause many issues in your system if your pipes are stagnant.

It is also likely that your pipes could get blocked if you do not protect the entrances and the exits. Now a person certainly does want the water to enter the pipes, but dirt and bugs are a big no-no. So, consider covering your drain pipes with a thin layer of cloth and consider using chicken wire for your exhaust pipes, especially if they happen to be close to the soil.

Be aware that most greenhouse fans are not designed for excessively humid environments. Many people have tried to build inline fans that work on DC power which leads to a solar panel. Yet time and again, many of these fans happen to fail merely after using it for a year. Now that will be quite expensive to have to replace the whole time, and should rather be avoided.

It is also best to be strategic with the automation system of your climate battery. It is so easy to have it run moderately or even inefficiently. You can consider operating your climate battery on a thermostat or even a smart controller, depending on where you purchase your products from.

Now, here are a few things you should consider doing with your climate battery, starting off with balancing the diameter of your pipe in order to let it run at its best. When you balance them out well, you can influence the amount of airflow energy that is stored, and just the whole heating and cooling system in general. It is also recommended that you use tools and items carefully. Whatever you decide to get will have an influence on how easy it is to install as well as the durability. Quality over quantity often applies in this matter, but do your research as well. Just because it is expensive doesn't mean it is always going to last. Stick with reliable brands, and even consider asking others who have greenhouses on which materials they used to build their climate battery if they have one. Finally, make sure the parts you get are easy to access again. This is a practical strategy to apply, considering that if your component breaks, you can easily have it replaced. However, the parts you install should hopefully last for years, if not decades, even depending on the quality.

Another factor you might not have thought about is noise. Certain fans can create a low, constant humming sound, and if it is close to your house, it might just turn out to be a huge annoyance. Therefore, make sure to select fans that have a reputation of being quiet, especially if the greenhouse is close to where you reside. Again, this is a small detail that can make all the difference in the world.

Floors

Now, it is obvious that your greenhouse does not need finished flooring, such as what you would find in a residential house. However, most of the area will be used for plants and depending on the plants and foundation, you may just have to level the surface. There are three different types of floors you can use for your greenhouse to plan accordingly.

The first-floor option is soil. This is when your greenhouse does not technically have a floor, and you can use gravel, wooden planks, or even pavers if need be for some walkways.

The second-floor option is stone, gravel, or pavers. They tend to work well with raised beds considering a person does not want to have any flooring materials directly underneath the beds.

The ideal scenario is to have insulated soil, in which the plants can spread their roots and thrive without suffering from frost either.

You can also consider using a concrete slab as your floor for your greenhouse. This has been a popular option, especially when you have a certain plan for your greenhouse. It brings alongside a number of benefits in comparison to the soil, gravel, or even stone. For instance, anything on wheels can easily be moved from place to place. It is not too far-fetched to bring and move a wheelbarrow, if at all necessary. It is certainly easier to keep clean and wash down. It can most certainly act as your foundation, and it is much easier to add a climate battery, as concrete not only creates an additional amount of thermal mass but also acts as a stabilizer. However, concrete can be quite costly, and you need to take this into consideration with your budget. A good idea is to get a quote from your local contractor in order to have a thorough understanding of how much it would cost you to install a concrete slab.

Keep in mind, a greenhouse is high in humidity, and anything contained inside should be humidity resistant, that includes the floor and multiple other items. The last thing you want is to have plant holders, tools, or even for the floor to rust or rot due to the natural humidity. Most people do not realize what water damage is. For a greenhouse, everything needs to be practically waterproof.

Importance of Drainage

Drainage plays a crucial role in your passive greenhouse, considering that if there is waterlogging, the damage can be quite serious. That is why it is recommended to build something called a French drain. If you have not heard of a French drain before, it is, in the simplest of terms, a drain pipe that is underground. The idea is to dig the pipe in at a certain angle. This prevents the surface area in your greenhouse from flooding and is possibly a good and affordable option to remove any waterlogged area in your greenhouse. The biggest advantage of it is its low price and simple design.

Building a drain pipe is not rocket science, and you do not necessarily need any special tools or massively complex equipment, but there are certain things you need to know and keep in mind.

The only thing you will need to figure out is where exactly you intend to dig the trench. Specifically, where the water will have direct access to. Keep in mind: you do not want to have the rainwater mix with the foul water drainage.

Foul drainage is water that is carrying properties, such as from washing machines, sinks, baths, and even toilets. When you mix the two up, you end up creating a high pollutant risk that is combined with very harmful chemicals. You can avoid this mistake by looking up the building regulations locally and checking out the planned drainage system.

So, how exactly do you install a French drain for your greenhouse? Firstly you start by digging two trenches. One could be the walking path in the middle of your greenhouse, and the other could be on the lower end of the wall right outside the greenhouse. It is best to keep your trench approximately three feet, or one meter, away from your building and make sure that the slope bottoms of your trench are facing downwards to a certain degree. It is recommended to have it drop about 0.25 per foot (M., 2018). You should also make sure the slope is pointed away from the greenhouse itself with about a minimum recommendation to have it at a 45 degrees angle. This creates the surety that all the soil that surrounds the trench is actually stable.

The next step would be to remain digging ditches at the end of the wall that is both in the greenhouse and outside. However, if you do happen to have a concrete slab as a foundation, that may be a little difficult for the inside, and some reconsideration will need to take place.

If you have dug the ditches at the end wall, you should eventually reach a time and point where the slope happens to drop off. This way, you can end the trenches at a slope and ratio of 1:50.

The third step would be to take your time lining any and all trenches with a drainage cloth, making sure it happens to cover all the sides and the bottom of the ditch completely. Then it is best to place a perforated drain pipe into your trench using couplings to connect all the necessary pieces. Make sure it is placed properly and cover it up with gravel. It should be completely covered, and you can finish it up by wrapping the gravel pipe. It would resemble a little bit of a hot dog, with the pipe being the sausage roll, the sauce being the gravel, and the cloth being the bread that covers the ditch. Afterward, finish your trench by covering the remaining layer with soil, and you will have a professional French drain that assists with the water.

Additional Heating

Now that you have fixed or set up a proper foundation as well as drainage, one can only wonder if there are any tips and tricks into adding any additional heating if needed. Additional heating is especially necessary if you live in a frigid environment, and the insulation alongside the thermal mass just might not be enough. These are common in polar climates, where you may struggle to collect enough solar energy.

When deciding to build a greenhouse, it is required to have a backup plan in regards to heat. How you are going to want to do it relies on a few factors, such as the options that exist, which you can use to heat up your greenhouse, and what is the absolute worst-case scenario when it comes to heating, as well as how much it may potentially cost you per year to have the heating. Having a backup plan takes away a little bit of the sole dependency you may have on the sun. Although solar is ideal, it can sometimes be unreliable for days to weeks, to the greenhouse's detriment.

When it comes to the options, you have a few. This includes using wood, a heat pump, natural gas, coal or oil, and perhaps even electricity. It is best to approach heating in a way that allows for maximum flexibility as well as staying as close to becoming a passive solar greenhouse as possible. It is important to have primary and backup heat sources. The greatest reason being is that if you were to leave your greenhouse for a couple of days (such as work or vacation), you would not want to have to be concerned about the temperature of the greenhouse. This is why it is good to have an automatic source that can turn on and off on its own while you are away. At the end of the day, while you are at home, you can use the cheapest forms of fuel, but when you decide to go away for a few days, then you do have a backup source that will kick in. This certainly works better than the alternative of having to get someone to babysit your greenhouse.

How exactly does this work? Consider that you have installed a wooden stove into your greenhouse that fuels on wood most of the time, but you have a natural gas heater installed as its backup if need be. Wood is certainly cheaper to get a hold of than gas and can burn for quite a while, but the gas can certainly be considered as the main backup source, as it doesn't need refueling on such a frequent basis. Building additional heating like this certainly takes the human factor into account. Most people need to go away from time to time and cannot be ever-present to attend to a greenhouse. Yet, at times, it seems to have the same realities of taking care of a dog. However, with a couple of backup plans, you will be reducing the amount of trouble hurdling your way.

Keep in mind that the backup system does tend to be a little colder than the optimal temperature, considering you are not always there to monitor it. For instance, you are using a wooden stove that allows the temperature to remain at 50 degrees Fahrenheit (10 celsius), but with your natural gas heater, it may only read about 40 degrees Fahrenheit (five celsius). Yet, if it works and keeps your plants healthy and happy, then there is no reason to be truly concerned. Plants typically have an ideal temperature range and will be okay with some mild variation caused by the backup system. If you can, work out the lowest temperature your greenhouse can reach that the plants will survive. This is done by calculating and figuring out the survivability of the plants.

Figuring Out Heat Loss in a Greenhouse

When figuring out the size of the heating that you need, the calculations can be quite complex and puzzling. More so, when you put in glazing, thermal mass, and other forms of building materials, all are contributing to the heat of the greenhouse. Therefore, the main principle is to gather enough information needed in order to properly calculate the surface area of your greenhouse as well as the glazing material that you have (the R-value) and the temperature you desire.

Then you would need to take the average of the coldest temperature outdoors during wintertime. There are also two primary ways in which heat is lost; one is through conduction, and the other is through infiltration.

Most of the heat loss happens through conduction. This tends to happen on the surface of the greenhouse, and you can also add a small amount of convection and radiation.

Therefore according to Bartok (2019), you can work it out to this equation: conductive heat loss + SA x U x TD.

SA happens to be the calculation of the glazed surface—you want to work out the total amount that is in exposure to the cold. You can work it out by calculating the areas of the sidewalls, endwalls, and roof.

The U represents the heat transfer from the glazing. Now according to Bartok (2019), (Btu/hr-sq ft - degree F) is how you work it out, but normally the value of an average single layer polycarbonate is 1.15 and 0.7 when it is a double layer. So it is about 0.6 if you are using acrylic or a double wall polycarbonate.

TD stands for the temperature difference, which is the highest temperature on a winter night. A good temperature as the norm for inside a greenhouse is recommended to be about 70 degrees Fahrenheit, but you can always look up your local area.

When working out the heat loss from inflation, you can use the formula: 0.02 x V x C x TD Bartok, 2019.

The V tends to stand for the total volume of your greenhouse, which is worked out through the multiplication of the area of the floor to the average estimated height of your building.

The C works out to be the number of air changes that occur in an hour. When it is a new greenhouse, consider using 0.5-1, and for a greenhouse that has been repaired and kept in high quality should be around 1.5. If the greenhouse is in a very poor and sad state, then a person has to make that figure about 2-3. If you are in a very windy location, then you have to add another 10% or even 5% to your answer.

Td stands for the same value in the previous equation that had been discussed. This happens to be the maximum temperature inside the greenhouse.

When you add the two formulas together, then you will have the total heat loss. It may be quite tricky and quite a lot of math, but it all plays a part in the success of your greenhouse. When you install a heating system, you need to have the output of the heating system to be preferably equal or, better yet, greater than the total heat loss you have calculated. Therefore, it is better to consider installing two small units. This creates a higher level of safety as well as a better form of efficiency for your greenhouse.

Using this tool can help prepare you for the worst-case scenario. It is certainly handy and saves you any pain that might come if the worst actually does happen. After all, setting up a plan is setting yourself up for success. Whereas failing to plan is planning to fail. After you have worked out the heaters you need, then you will be able to work out the costs for the year quite easily, including fuel costs, and maybe add potential repairs if need be.

Integrating Your Design

The best part about custom designing your greenhouse is placing in elements that are unique and not commonly found in an average greenhouse to truly personalize your greenhouse. Yet working well and smart can allow for a smooth and successful integration of the different elements.

Defining Permaculture

A person can easily determine the needs, yields, and characteristics that are intrinsic to an element. The needs are practically the tools you use in order for something to work or survive. The yields or the products are the plants you get to grow in the greenhouse, and the intrinsic characteristics focus all on the different traits. For a passive solar greenhouse, it needs heat, insulation, and a certain amount of ventilation. Depending on your region, as well as the plants you want to grow, it will impact the characteristics you want in your passive solar greenhouse by the end of the day. All of these are parts of permaculture. You can use the same process of figuring out the parts of the elements in order to work out the best and most efficient way to infiltrate and build your greenhouse, specifically when it comes to heating.

To put it as simply as possible, everything that a person creates has certain needs and yields. For example, you cannot stack and organize paper neatly together without a folder or run a car without fuel. Your job for the passive solar greenhouse is to work out all these characteristics in order to build on the success of your own custom design.

You can consider designing as matchmaking. Find a part that needs another piece in order to play a certain role in your greenhouse. A person can break every single element down into practical needs for you to work out, specifically into needs and yields, which can be the first wise step into the design.

The elements that could be considered to be installed into a passive solar greenhouse could be a sauna, wood-fired hot tub, root cellar, or even solar dehydrator. So there is really no true limit to what you could add to your passive solar greenhouse.

Furthermore, if you intend to add your greenhouse to your home, you need to keep it in mind before the vapor and humidity. Yet this is not impossible. Rather, you can use items in your house such as stale air, exhaust from the heat recovery ventilator, or even the bathroom fans. Your house will get extra space in regards to the greenhouse as well as a "grocery" store of free food literally a door away.

At the end of the day, extra heating is important, especially if you are in a region that has frigid winters. A passive solar greenhouse is not too difficult, but it has some complicated moments. That is why it is better to take your time planning and customizing your greenhouse according to what it would suit best. Keep in mind all the characteristics and plan everything before you even start with the construction. You should make sure to add all the important elements of a greenhouse and then some. Don't forget to discuss with local greenhouse producers, as they will have a load of valuable advice specifically about the environment and materials. You will find how incredibly rewarding the journey is once everything has been set up and you have yourself a greenhouse and self-sustaining food. Now with a basic plan, understanding of the important elements, all that is left is to build it. Yet where to start? This is practically the part when you put everything you have truly learned into practice and consider working just a little outside the box.

Chapter 7:
Construction Steps

Now that you have the foundational knowledge, it is time to take the next big step and move into the actual DIY and planning. You know the primary aspects to focus on, but it is great to have a general idea of what you should do and the steps you need to take in order to succeed in building a passive solar greenhouse. We estimated that it can take about a month to build your greenhouse. Be aware, this is a guideline, and you can tweak it to your own time and tools if you need to.

Tools You Will Need

Basic construction tools are a must-have. These items are especially important for DIY, and if you are missing some of these tools, you may need to go shopping first:

- Screwdriver Set

- Tape Measure

- Toolbox

- Hammer

- Duct Tape

- Flashlight

- Set of Pliers

- Utility Knife

- Putty Knife

- Handsaw

- Adjustable Wrench

- Shovel

The next step would be to figure out the ingredients of your greenhouse itself. What materials are you going to use to build it with? What glazing are you going to use? Are you going to install ventilation systems?

Write down a list of all the tools and material you will need to start. Then, check to see what you already have and what you need. You might only need to buy some of the materials after all the excessive planning is done. So, both gathering your tools and the planning of your greenhouse do come hand in hand.

Common Materials

Every greenhouse is unique. Still, as a beginner, it can be hard to know where to start when shopping for materials. Therefore, this is a generalized list to get you going. But be aware, depending on your customizations, some materials may not be needed while others may have to be added to the list.

- Pillars or reinforcement: iron, aluminum, galvanized steel, wood

- Straps or beams: iron, galvanized steel, aluminum

- Arches: aluminum, galvanized steel

- In foundation, foundation bases, or supports: concrete

- Securing of the cover: galvanized wires, aluminum, or steel that has been galvanized

- Canals: aluminum or steel that has been galvanized

- Crop wire: aluminum, galvanized wire, steel

Covers:

- Plastic Film

- Rigid plastics

- Glass

Keep in mind these are the most common materials and perhaps would not cover everything according to what you want (depending on your customized and personal greenhouse), but it gives you a general idea of what you may need to get.

Budget Estimation

The budget depends on where you live and the cost of materials when you get them. However, according to *The Passive Solar Greenhouse* (n.d.), here are some of the cost estimations. Again, keep in mind, it will vary from where you come from and labor costs. On average, total material costs are normally about $8,150 Us dollars, or $7,000 dollars (this excludes solar fans, panels, cistern, spigot, and cistern foundation/pad).

Normally, if you are unskilled in construction, you may need some labor help, such as a carpenter and a skilled helper that can work part-time. However, if you are well equipped enough yourself or have friends to lend a hand, then labor costs will be cut out for the most part (excluding an electrician or any services that do require a licensed professional). So, labor costs could be about $6,150 or less. Of course, this also depends on your area.

The totals given are if you intend to build a high-quality greenhouse, but there is the possibility to build passive solar greenhouses that are significantly lower.

Steps to Your Solar Passive Greenhouse

Week One:

Step One: Goal Setting

Time to set your goals. The best way to turn your goals into a legitimate design is by asking yourself the primary question: which climate do you want to imitate?

Depending on the zone, you will have to focus on the different temperatures. A good method of calculating the material you will need to create the zone you want is by asking professionals such as a mechanical engineer or a local greenhouse designer. Otherwise, you can consider using tools such as the USDA Design Tool online for a fee. Unless you are a mechanical engineer of your own, you may need help working out how to build your customized climate for your passive greenhouse. So, take your time working it out, as it is a foundational step into building your greenhouse.

Step Two: Location

Now, you have to figure out the location of your site. It is an obvious step, as you need to now work out the best positioning for your greenhouse in order to absorb the highest amount of solar radiation if possible. Take your first week making all the calculations and blueprints as explained in the previous chapters.

Step Three: Determine the Shape

This works alongside step two. After you have found the location, it is best to work out your aspect ratio and determine the shape or possibly even cross-section of your greenhouse. All of these are quite flexible and certainly need to be customized to your specific needs, layout, and goals determined beforehand. This is why it is best to do all the planning and choices within the first week.

Step Four: Order Materials

Order the necessary, customized material needed to start, whether it is the pipes for the underground climate battery, or the concrete for the foundation, or even just the metal frames. It is now time to order and customize your material in order to get started on week two. Where you are and what materials are immediately available also determines the time frame in which this will be built.

Week Two:

Step Five: Foundation Beginnings

Now, it is time to build your foundation. Considering this is a very critical step, it can take a few days to even a week to accomplish (especially if you are pouring out concrete which needs a few days of rest afterward). You need to plan its layout as well as consider all the variations and steps you would want to implement. Do you want a climate battery? If so, then you may want to plan for the pipes, fans, and installation. If you want to have a concrete slab alongside it, then add that to the plan. Keep in mind that you want to make absolutely sure the foundation is below the frost line. If you do not do this, you could have your frames twisting, and if you have glass, it will shatter. This is beyond disastrous and can be avoided if you just dig a little deeper. If you intend to pour a concrete slab, then make it at least four inches deep. You also need to dig a trench that is below the frost line and then pour it into your concrete wall. Otherwise, it may not support the weight of the greenhouse.

Foundation for Solar Passive Greenhouse buildings

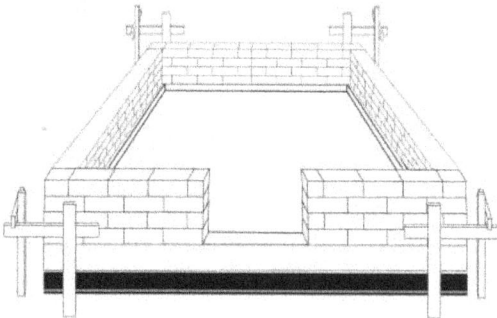

Be sure to rent any tools needed for digging. Even if you don't intend to build a climate battery, you may still have considered installing a French drain, and yet again, this involves laying a pipeline underground. So, be sure to have everything you planned ready when working on the foundation, as installing anything underground now is quite important and convenient before any form of the foundation has yet to be applied.

You could also build your greenhouse on an existing wooden deck, as long as the footings are placed below your frost line. You also need to check that the framing and posts are in good condition as well as resistant to rot since a greenhouse is all about humidity. The last thing you want is your greenhouse to crumble within a couple of months due to weak moldy wood.

Depending on your foundation, you will have a factor in a certain amount of time. If you start with no foundation, then the holes for the framework and the building are all that you need to be concerned about, and you can have it done within a day or two. Start off by measuring the footprint which your frame will occupy. If you do lay a foundation, it is best to plan this to be done in a week. Therefore, the next step-framing comes in week three.

Week Three:

Step Six: Greenhouse Framework

As you are laying your foundation, it is best to make your orders on the framework, making sure it is all customized and ready within the third week when you intend to start off. Your plans of both ventilation and insulation should also be considered and will be installed along week three and week four.

Once you have prepared the space on the ground, as well as the foundation, it is now time to secure your frames to the base of your greenhouse. You will have to choose a certain style or frame that matches your foundation. This is a very important step for building your greenhouse, and it results in the functionality as well as efficiency of your entire project. This is why it is best to look up the different styles and frames beforehand in order to be completely sure of your decision, making sure it meets your budget. You will be placing the frames alongside the perimeter, bolting them down. If you need extra strength, you can secure steel cables in the X bracing shape to add to the security and strength against the wind and other external factors that might push the limit of your greenhouse. You want to make sure the foundation and the framework are sturdy from the start.

Greenhouse Frameworks

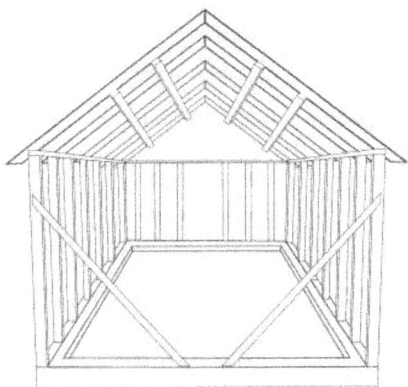

Once you have finished with the framework (the skeleton), it is time to double-check that everything is secured. This is inspecting the joints and all the connections. You want to look for any potentially harmful sharp points or rough spots that might harm the plastic sheet that goes over the frame. Using an angle grinder, you can smooth down any of these points. If you do not have the tool, then you could simply use soft fabric to wrap them instead. This will act as a cushion for the rest of your material.

Once you have the frame and structure set up, you will be focusing on your doors and hardware. You need to make sure you have both an entry and exit that works and fits with your greenhouse theme.

There are a vast majority of door options and can also be insulated if you want to add to the R-value of your greenhouse. Make sure you get the proper nuts, bolts, and brackets to make it strong and have the ability to endure harsh storm conditions.

Your next step will be choosing your covering and applying. This is normally the glazing materials, as has been discussed before. There are a variety of materials available of various thicknesses and different R-values. Again, make sure you have a great understanding of how much light and insulation you want before installing it into your greenhouse. Finally, make sure everything is properly sealed. This can normally be done all within a week. Make sure any necessary appointments are also made within this week, such as with an electrician if need be as well as proper ventilation.

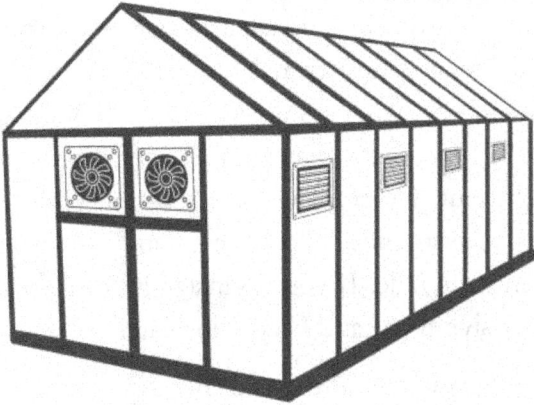

Week Four:

Your last week will be installing the last important parts of your greenhouse, such as the glazing. Then, in week three, the glazing needs to be ordered and customized according to the frames that you installed. This might take some more time, depending on the form of glazing you want. So, keep in mind that this can take a week or even more if the material you need is not immediately available.

Considering the covering makes or breaks your greenhouse after the frame, you want to make absolutely sure it is properly installed. The ideal installation would be that you do not receive any wind or leaks into your greenhouse. When applying your glazing, it is always recommended to build on a double layer. If you install a single layer, you have to do so at your own risk, especially if you are in a tougher climate. You want to introduce an air bubble for extra insulation, but strength is also important. Keep in mind, again, that glass always looks aesthetically pleasing, and plastic does eventually fade. If you do install glass, do yourself a massive favor and keep it insulated.

Step Seven: Installing the Glazing

Installing glazing is not too complicated as long as you make the frames square and level. Normally, a good kit will come with glazing tape as well as caulking and an aluminum barcap. This seals your glazing tightly, making it waterproof and far better insulated. Glazing tape works like putty because you will find it to be sticky on either side. You can start by unrolling your tape and pressing it tightly against the bars. Then you position your glazing and slowly but surely press it against the tape. Then you can use the butyl caulking on the edges of your glazing as well as installing the barcaps. The role of barcaps is to keep your glazing in place.

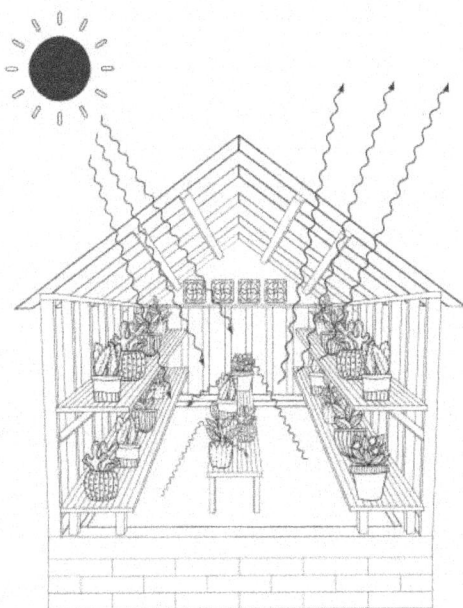

Step Eight: Installing the Ventilation and Heating

Your next step would be to place both the cooling as well as the ventilation. Then, you can decide to add shading to your greenhouse, passive ventilation, mechanical, or both. This can take a day or two to install, depending on the difficulty. You might also have to hire someone depending on the regulations of your country. So, remember to plan and bring in a licensed electrician when you need to install anything electrical.

Step Nine: Heating System

Once you have completed step eight, it is time to decide upon your heating system. After the ventilation, take your time installing the heating according to the plans you have selected prior, all customized for your greenhouse. Again, it is better to install two variations of heating. One with cheaper fuel and the other as a backup system, especially if you cannot afford to attend your greenhouse every day. It might seem easy at first, but the moment you are required to do it on a daily basis, you will not be able to go on vacation or go away for the weekend. You don't want your greenhouse to be your prison, so make sure you choose an appropriately sized heating system.

Step Ten: Environmental Controls

The next step will be to place your environmental controls such as thermostats or even computer modules and a misting system if need be. Make sure the items you install are user-friendly. It may not be all that necessary, and this is more of a luxury than a necessity, but when you install automated systems, it does create a more passive solar greenhouse with less labor work. However, again, it all depends on your budget and what you are indeed able to afford.

In Conclusion

Now that you have installed your foundation, insulation, ventilation, and temperature, as well as climate control, you are well on your way to a successful greenhouse. Feel free to add anything else you had in mind, including the containers for your plants or the gravel for your walkways if you have soil for your floor. You could consider a greenhouse bench, curtains for insulating your glazing, or even blanket cloths for your plants. Of course, all this depends on your budget and what you can afford at the end of the day. Now, you have a clear idea of the plan you need to formulate and the steps to constructing your greenhouse. It is not so complicated after all.

When building your first greenhouse, however, keep things as simple as possible, especially if it is your first time. The more complicated it gets, the more time you should give yourself to set things right. Of all the installations, the foundation may take you the most time, especially if you add concrete, considering that concrete needs time to cure. Yet if you give your greenhouse enough time and attention, then you will have it up and running in no time.

Maintenance of Your Greenhouse

Since you are planning on running your greenhouse throughout the year, you will have to pay attention to maintenance after construction, as everything in the greenhouse can get dirty and attract other problems which just might come your way. Since soil is a major component in a greenhouse, it will get on everything and will sneak onto multiple surfaces and crevices. Whereas water evaporates, leaving condensation on glass or other surfaces. All of these can start to attract fungi as well as draw in unwanted pests.

The best way to maintain and keep your greenhouse clean is by jet-washing or power washing when your greenhouse is empty. Now, if you have pots, it is easy enough to move them outside as you quickly clear and clean your greenhouse. Or you can get someone to work with a disinfectant for you. When using a disinfectant, pick one that is harmless to the plants you are growing but tackles the unwanted mold and pests that come in from time to time.

You also need to be prepared for faulty equipment in the greenhouse, as materials do not last forever, and sometimes they are just poorly manufactured. It means, however, you need to keep a lookout for problems and fix them as quickly as possible before they negatively affect your plants. For example, when it comes to heaters, you need to watch out for corrosion. This is a huge indication of pipe leakage, and you want to fix it as soon as possible.

It would help if you also considered checking all the ventilation equipment such as doors, fans, and window seals every season. This is because many of them have the nasty knack of breaking down with wear and tear and abrupt changes in the weather. If you are using screens for your greenhouse, regularly check for tears and potential holes. The last thing you want is it coming apart on a bad day. It is best to keep them clear of dirt and any gunge that may build up from time to time with the fans. As you want to prevent breakages from blockages, and if you have a misting system, be sure to keep a lookout for leaks and cracks. This is normally trickier, considering that water moves away normally from the guilty spot.

If you have glass for glazing, then keep an eye out for any cracked or potential broken glass. If you find any, it is best to replace them as soon as you spot them. Considering these gaps can let pests inside, and if water freezes inside, it cracks it and makes things infinitely worse. Make sure to check the entirety of your greenhouse, especially after a bad storm. A good rule of thumb is to look for corrosion or potential breaks in the metal itself.

The places and spots in your greenhouse that you don't normally visit also need to be inspected. Making sure there are no cracks, leaks, or even signs of gnawing if you happen to have wires. Any system that may only be used on a seasonal basis should be checked regularly to see if it works, specifically any backup systems, such as your heaters.

The best way to prevent many of your problems is by adding a routine inspection into your schedule, once a week or a month. Make sure to create a suitable routine that works for you and your lifestyle and put it into practice. Just as you have built your greenhouse, you now have to maintain it, as nothing lasts forever, and accidents do happen. You want to stop a problem before it gets big, however, and this is why inspections are so very important to the overall efficiency of your passive solar-powered greenhouse.

Conclusion

Now you have come to the end of the line. Finally, you have the information and a plan to get you started in your solar passive greenhouse journey. This involves more than gardening, but you build yourself something better than a simple garden; you build a self-sustaining, eco-friendly environment for plants to thrive year-round. Building greenhouses should undoubtedly be encouraged worldwide, reducing the necessity of surviving on chemicalized foods and creating plant-friendly environments right at your back door. You may be a little overwhelmed by all the information, but there is no need to stress. Simply go back and review where necessary, building yourself a careful plan before going on ahead into construction. As the saying goes, slow but steady does win the race after all.

When building a passive solar greenhouse, you will need to remember the four key elements:

1. Orientation, as the placement of your greenhouse is fundamental.

2. Insulation is key to keeping your greenhouse warm and safe in the winter.

3. Ventilation works for reducing heat and adding humidity in the summer.

4. Temperature and climate control.

It may be drilled a couple of times, but they are the building blocks to a successful greenhouse. Sure, there are other elements you can add on, but in reality, without these four, your greenhouse is not likely to succeed.

Balance is also crucial because it is possible to have too much of something. There could be too much ventilation or too much light, or even too much insulation. Yet, the polar opposite can also be a problem. Working out your balance amongst these elements is moving ahead and thinking smart.

Yet, your budget may determine what you can and cannot afford or what your plans are. Keep in mind that, often, cheaper purchases lead to more work, which will negate any costs you would have saved upfront. You need to decide what you can manage on your busy schedule and even consider your plans for the year ahead. It is easy to commit from the start, but it is more a marathon than a sprint when it comes to a greenhouse and growing plants all year long. Keeping a greenhouse is practically like keeping a pet. You need to work out all the advantages, disadvantages, needs, and categories it falls under.

Furthermore, if you do not have the knowledge or are not entirely sure about questions and facts regarding your environment, do not be afraid to ask for help or information. You are bound to be surprised by the various tips and tricks people may show you. You could even consider joining online communities available on Facebook, as they are more open to answering questions as well as helping you out should you face any problems. Communities are there for a reason, and why not take advantage of the knowledge of people who have gone and built greenhouses before you? Specifically, reach out to those that have built In your area and climate and are accustomed to the limitations and requirements.

Be detailed with your planning and do your research on the items you need for your greenhouse. It is best to make your choices of the glazing, ventilation system, foundation, and multiple other criteria before even starting your construction, as many of the items need to be installed at the same time or at least prepared for them. Some things even need to be custom designed depending on your plans, and you need to adapt to that. Make sure the items you want are also easily obtainable.

Now that you are equipped with all the tools and knowledge, it is time to go out and use them to the best of your ability. Keep in mind to think a little out of the box and to customize the knowledge to your specific needs, location, goals, and intentions. For example, going for a passive solar greenhouse is shaving off a lot of money and creating a far better and self-sustaining environment than multiple other greenhouses built. Not only are you doing yourself a big favor, but you are genuinely participating in bettering the environment while providing for yourself your own food! If that is not incredibly exciting, then what is?

The journey ends here, and you have the necessary tools to proceed on your own. It may seem like a daunting journey, but this is a gratifying project that will not only benefit you, the community as a whole.

References

Arcadia GlassHouse. (n.d.). *Tip #11: Does My Greenhouse Need a Permit?* Arcadia GlassHouse. https://arcadiaglasshouse.com/greenhouse-tips/tip-11-greenhouse-need-permit/

Avis, R. (2018a, March 29). *How to Design a Passive Solar Greenhouse: Setting Goals, Site Selection, Aspect Ratio and Shape, —Part 1 of 4.* Medium. https://medium.com/@rob_74123/how-to-design-a-passive-solar-greenhouse-part-1-of-3-8c08ccbfbde8

Avis, R. (2018b, March 30). *How to Design a Passive Solar Greenhouse: Foundations, Kneewall, Ventilation & Glazing, —Part 2 of 4.* Medium. https://medium.com/@rob_74123/how-t0-design-a-passive-solar-greenhouse-part-2-of-4-e41471ab06e6

Avis, R. (2018c, March 31). *How to Design a Passive Solar Greenhouse: Light, Insulation and Subterranean Heating and Cooling, —Part 3 of 4.* Medium. https://medium.com/@rob_74123/how-to-design-a-passive-solar-greenhouse-light-insulation-and-subterranean-heating-and-cooling-7c66a27afd29

Barth, B. (2018, July 17). *DIY Misting System for Your Greenhouse, Barn, or Patio Party.* Modern Farmer. https://modernfarmer.com/2018/07/diy-misting-system-for-your-greenhouse-barn-or-patio-party/

Bartok, J. (2019, July 17). *Determining greenhouse heat loss.* Greenhouse Management. https://www.greenhousemag.com/article/technology-determining-greenhouse-heat-loss/

Bradford Research Center. (n.d.). *Passive Solar Greenhouse.* Bradford.missouri.edu; University of Missouri. https://bradford.missouri.edu/passive-solar-greenhouse/

Ceres Greenhouse Solutions. (2015a, January 21). *Solar Greenhouse Basics: Ventilation.* Ceres GS. https://ceresgs.com/solar-greenhouse-basics-ventilation/

Ceres Greenhouse Solutions. (2015b, February 24). *3 Types of Greenhouse Floors.* Ceres GS. https://ceresgs.com/3-types-of-greenhouse-floors/

Ceres Greenhouse Solutions. (2017, July 3). *How to Choose a Glazing Material for a Year Round Greenhouse.* Ceres GS. https://ceresgs.com/how-t0-choose-a-glazing-material-for-a-year-round-greenhouse/

Ceres Greenhouse Solutions. (2021, April 18). *10 Do's and Don'ts for Designing a Ground to Air Heat Transfer System*. Ceres GS. https://ceresgs.com/10-dos-and-donts-for-designing-a-ground-to-air-heat-transfer-system/

Claney, K. (2016, December 25). *Top 3 Problems When Installing Polygal (Multi-wall Polycarbonate)*. Regal Plastics Blog. https://www.regal-plastics.com/blog/top-3-problems-associated-with-improper-polygal-installation/

Garden & Greenhouse. (2012, June 5). *The Basics of Greenhouse Ventilation*. Garden & Greenhouse. https://www.gardenandgreenhouse.net/articles/greenhouse-articles/the-basics-of-greenhouse-venilation/

Greenhouse Emporium. (2019, April 8). *What You Need to Know About Greenhouse Insulation*. Greenhouse Emporium. https://greenhouseemporium.com/blogs/greenhouse-gardening/greenhouse-insulation/

Kosimov, S. (n.d.). *Central Asian Countries Initiative for Land Management*. Cacilm. http://www.cacilm.org/en/technologies/section/greenhouse/solar

M., A. (2018, March 1). *A Complete Guide to Greenhouse Drainage*. Greenhouse Growing.

https://www.growingreenhouse.com/greenhouse-drainage/

Machnich, C. (2019, August 9). *How to Create the Ideal Ventilation System for Your Greenhouse.* Greenhouse Grower. https://www.greenhousegrower.com/technology/how-to-create-the-ideal-ventilation-system-for-your-greenhouse/

Meuse, J. (2018, September 11). *Constructing a Home Greenhouse.* FineGardening. https://www.finegardening.com/article/constructing-a-home-greenhouse

Mistcooling. (2015, December 25). *Why a Greenhouse Misting System is Worth Installing?* Mistcooling Blog. https://www.mistcooling.com/blog/why-a-greenhouse-misting-system-is-worth-installing/

Nelson, L. (2019, October 9). *7 Things to Know Before Building a Greenhouse.* Lawnstarter. https://www.lawnstarter.com/blog/landscaping/7-things-to-know-before-building-a-greenhouse/

Quinn, M. (2014, September 7). *How to Avoid the Most Common Greenhouse Mistakes.* Gardener's Path. https://gardenerspath.com/how-to/greenhouses-and-coldframes/avoid-common-greenhouse-mistakes/

Roe, B. (2017, January 31). *Greenhouse Misting: Creating the Best Environment.* Koolfog. https://koolfog.com/greenhouse-misting-creating-best-environment/

Schiller, L. (2016, November 29). *Climate Control and Your Year-Round Solar Greenhouse.* GreenBuilders Media. https://www.greenbuildermedia.com/blog/climate-control-and-your-year-round-solar-greenhouse#:~:text=The%20most%20common%20climate%20control

Scijinks. (n.d.). *What Are the Different Climate Types?* Scijinks.gov. https://scijinks.gov/climate-zones

Storey, A. (2017, September 12). *How to Decipher Heat Loss and Greenhouse R-Value.* Upstart University. https://university.upstartfarmers.com/blog/decipher-heat-loss-r-value-greenhouse#:~:text=And%20anyone%20who%20has%20begun

The Editors of Encyclopedia Britannica. (2019). Latent Heat. *Encyclopedia Britannica.* https://www.britannica.com/science/latent-heat

The Greenhouse Catalogue. (n.d.). *Greenhouse Kits and Greenhouse and Garden Supplies.* Greenhouse Catalogue.

https://www.greenhousecatalog.com/greenhouse-ventilation

Thoma, M. (2020, July 25). *7 Useful Features You Need in a Passive Solar Greenhouse.* Healthy Fresh Homegrown. https://tranquilurbanhomestead.com/passive-solar-greenhouse/#insulate_the_north_wall

United States Department of Agriculture. (n.d.). *USDA Plant Hardiness Zone Map.* Plant Hardiness. https://planthardiness.ars.usda.gov/PHZMWeb/Maps.aspx

Image References

Aesthetic Greenhouse ninikvaratskhelia_. (2020, April 27). Greenhouse Flowers Blossom. Pixabay.com. https://pixabay.com/photos/greenhouse-flowers-blossom-bloom-5095328/

Best To Install Your Glazing In Even Squares/ Rectangular Structure La coccinelle. (2019, November 24). white metal stand in yard. Unsplash. https://unsplash.com/photos/ozXAKOBDkK4

Cold Climates Marek Okon. (2019, December 20). snow-covered trees beside body of water. Unsplash. https://unsplash.com/photos/ZNZ6EQscVw4

Common Example of a Kneewall Tiago Lopes. (2020, August 21). white and brown wooden house near green trees during daytime. Unsplash. https://unsplash.com/photos/45YovdnShwg

Example of Passive Ventilation www.zanda. photography. (2018, January 18). green watering can in green house. Unsplash. https://unsplash.com/photos/RBdE3jv5y68

Foundation Beginnings Blake, S. (2021, January 8). aerial view of gray concrete building. Unsplash. https://unsplash.com/photos/rsGd-rXFGkM

Greenhouse Framework Duncan, H. (2018, February 15). empty abandoned house at daytime. Unsplash.
https://unsplash.com/photos/R4LfI6sygvw

Greenhouse With an Insulated Wall Harits Mustya Pratama. (2019, February 24). green vegetables. Unsplash.   https://unsplash.com/photos/F47-qMQzVwQ

Greenhouse Glazing Materials Spratt, A. (2019, November 7). people inside greenhouse. Unsplash. https://unsplash.com/photos/YJGhQxiYWt8

Ventilation is Important inkanoack. (2014, July 14). Fan Fresh Air Greenhouse - Free photo on Pixabay.   Pixabay.com. https://pixabay.com/photos/fan-fresh-air-greenhouse-technology-388937/

www.ingramcontent.com/pod-product-compliance
Lightning Source LLC
Chambersburg PA
CBHW060051100426
42742CB00014B/2779